BEST PRACTICES

—— ARE ——

STUPID

BEST PRACTICES

— ARE —

STUPID

40 WAYS
TO OUT-INNOVATE
THE COMPETITION

STEPHEN M. SHAPIRO

PORTFOLIO / PENGUIN

PORTFOLIO / PENGUIN
Published by the Penguin Group
Penguin Group (USA) Inc., 375 Hudson Street, New York, New York 10014, U.S.A. • Penguin Group (Canada), 90 Eglinton Avenue East, Suite 700, Toronto, Ontario, Canada M4P 2Y3 (a division of Pearson Penguin Canada Inc.) • Penguin Books Ltd, 80 Strand, London WC2R 0RL, England • Penguin Ireland, 25 St. Stephen's Green, Dublin 2, Ireland (a division of Penguin Books Ltd) • Penguin Books Australia Ltd, 250 Camberwell Road, Camberwell, Victoria 3124, Australia (a division of Pearson Australia Group Pty Ltd) • Penguin Books India Pvt Ltd, 11 Community Centre, Panchsheel Park, New Delhi—110 017, India • Penguin Group (NZ), 67 Apollo Drive, Rosedale, Auckland 0632, New Zealand (a division of Pearson New Zealand Ltd) • Penguin Books (South Africa) (Pty) Ltd, 24 Sturdee Avenue, Rosebank, Johannesburg 2196, South Africa

Penguin Books Ltd, Registered Offices: 80 Strand, London WC2R 0RL, England

First published in 2011 by Portfolio / Penguin, a member of Penguin Group (USA) Inc.

10 9 8 7 6 5 4 3

Illustrations by Juraj Chrastina

LIBRARY OF CONGRESS CATALOGING-IN-PUBLICATION DATA
Shapiro, Stephen M., 1964–
Best practices are stupid : 40 ways to out-innovate the competition / Stephen M. Shapiro.
p. cm.
Includes bibliographical references and index.
ISBN 978-1-59184-385-6 (hardback)
1. Organizational change. 2. Organizational change—Management. 3. Organizational effectiveness.
4. Creative ability in business. I. Title.
HD58.8.S4775 2011
658.4'063—dc22
2011016153

Printed in the United States of America
Designed by Carla Bolte

While the author has made every effort to provide accurate telephone numbers and Internet addresses at the time of publication, neither the publisher nor the author assumes any responsibility for errors, or for changes that occur after publication. Further, publisher does not have any control over and does not assume any responsibility for author or third-party Web sites or their content.

As always, to my parents and sister . . .
the best family in the world.

CONTENTS

STRATEGY
Innovation Strategy and Customers

MEASURES
Innovation Measures and Motivation

PEOPLE
Organization, Leadership, and Culture

CREATIVITY
Techniques for Stimulating Creative Thinking

BEST PRACTICES

—— ARE ——

STUPID

INTRODUCTION

On April 20, 2010, the environment was dealt a horrific blow. On that day, the Deepwater Horizon oil rig exploded, spewing as much as 180 million gallons of crude oil into the waters off the Gulf Coast of the United States. It took eighty-seven days to cap the gushing wellhead.

In the weeks following the explosion, scientists, movie stars, and concerned citizens tried to devise ways to slow the flow. But workable solutions were hard to find and implement, as the well was nearly a mile below the surface of the ocean. Repeated attempts failed.

In an effort to find better solutions, the Deepwater Horizon Unified Command, spearheaded by BP, launched a Web site where anyone could submit their ideas in an online suggestion box. According to *USA Today*, the Web site received nearly 125,000 ideas; 80,000 suggestions had to do with plugging the leak and 43,000 with ways to clean up the oil.

Of these ideas, one hundred were deemed to have some merit and a couple dozen were tested.

On the surface, this might appear to have been a successful endeavor; BP was able to gather lots of possible ideas to help end the disaster.

For a company that stood to lose billions of dollars in cleanup costs, relief payouts, and lost sales due to bad publicity, this approach might indeed have been a good strategy.

But the resources necessary to respond to this type of disaster typically don't exist within organizations. Although a workable solution may have been found using this strategy, it is unclear whether that was the case. Regardless, consider how many people it would take to evaluate thousands of ideas. If one person could evaluate an idea in thirty seconds (which is optimistic, especially for a technically complex issue like this) and could dedicate forty hours a week to the task, it would take over half a year to evaluate that many submissions, a significant investment for any company.

With an innovation strategy like this, finding a useful idea is like finding a needle in a haystack. Or more accurately, it is like finding a needle in a stack of other needles.

Unfortunately, this innovation strategy is what many well-intentioned companies use in their quest to be more innovative. They operate under the misguided belief that getting more ideas leads to better innovation. Organizations that use this approach spend a lot of their time sorting the wheat from the chaff. And sadly, most of the ideas are chaff.

As this book will reveal, you don't want more ideas. You want to focus your energies on finding solutions to pressing problems that enable your company to be more innovative. In fact, I'll teach you why the key to innovating *successfully* involves innovating *efficiently*.

The popular press and innovation gurus alike often provide well-worn examples that muddy the waters on how to approach the innovation process.

Google reportedly lets its employees use 20 percent of their time to develop new ideas. "PhDs and other smarty pants agreed to hand over their brains to the search giant for four days of the week and, in return, they were given the fifth to work on any project of their fancy." Many experts hold this up as an effective way to innovate. In actuality, this investment was designed to help Google win the "war for talent" and did little in the way of generating new revenue streams. In spite of the huge investment, 97 percent of its revenues still come from advertising, the same way it has always made money.

3M uses a similar strategy, giving employees 15 percent of their time to explore. When discussing the 15 percent rule, someone from 3M once told me, "Which fifteen percent? I work sixty hours a week and there's no time for my fifteen percent." The answer appears to involve working weekends. As Les Krogh, retired senior vice president of research and development, once said, "If 3Mers have to get something done, they'll do it. They'll take their 15 percent on Saturdays or Sundays, if need be."

Admittedly, 3M's approach has indeed produced some amazing innovations. But will this strategy work for your organization? Both Google and 3M benefit from a highly motivated workforce that is probably more ambitious than employees in most organizations.

So is there a more efficient way for you to innovate?

Allowing employees to dedicate 15 percent to 20 percent of their time to the innovation efforts of their choosing is akin to the infinite monkey theorem: If you give an infinite number of monkeys an infinite number of typewriters, they will eventually write *War and Peace*. The belief is that if you give employees enough time to tinker around and develop enough harebrained ideas, they will eventually find the next big innovation (and no, I am not suggesting that your employees are monkeys).

Although this might yield new ideas, it is hardly an efficient way to innovate.

Let's face it, the old models of innovation are broken, are inefficient, and fail to produce results.

It's time for you to be innovative about the way you innovate and apply some new thinking to your innovation process.

This book is composed of forty tips designed to help you do just that. These tips are designed to help you innovate differently. Innovate more efficiently. Innovate in a more focused manner.

Some tips are intended to change the way you think about innovation. Others are designed to change how you innovate. Depending on your experience level, you may already be familiar with some tips, while others will be new concepts for even the most advanced innovation practitioners. Certain tips are useful mainly at an organizational level, while others are important concepts for all individuals to consider.

In some cases, you may not agree with my point of view. That's okay! The objective of each tip is to get you and your team thinking. You don't necessarily need to take what I say at face value. Challenge each concept. Discuss it. See how it applies to your organization. There is no one-size-fits-all solution for innovation. Pick and choose the tips that will have the greatest impact.

Although the tips are organized in a logical sequence, they

can be read in any order and each stands on its own. The first series of tips introduces some of the most important concepts relating to "innovating the way you innovate," and the remainder of the book is loosely organized around the components of the innovation capability: process, strategy, measures, people, and technology:

- *Process:* Most innovation efforts are ineffective and unfocused. To remedy this, you will be introduced to challenge-driven innovation, an efficient process for addressing your most pressing issues and opportunities.
- *Strategy:* If you don't understand your customers' latent desires, your innovation efforts will be comparable to a wild-goose chase. Armed with their true wants and needs, you can develop a powerful innovation strategy.
- *Measures:* Your measurement systems may inadvertently be killing your innovation efforts. By making some simple changes to your motivation strategy, you can stimulate creativity and foster innovation.
- *People:* Innovation is dependent on having the right people—with divergent points of view—in the right roles. The key is to treat each individual like an owner of the business, pushing decision making to the lowest levels of the organization.
  - *Creativity:* One aspect of the people dimension is competency. With innovation, one specific competency involves the ability to develop creative solutions. Although creativity is technically part of the "people" dimension of the innovation capability, given its importance, I have dedicated a section to these techniques. These can be used in

brainstorming sessions or as instructional aids for helping people be more creative.

- *Technology:* Technology plays a critical role in finding solutions to challenges and enabling collaboration. Although this is a distinct component of the innovation capability, the world of technology is changing rapidly. Therefore, anything written in a book would be immediately obsolete. As a result, appendix A contains an overview of the technology landscape, and the most up-to-date information can be found on our Web site.

I am always amazed by the high quality of people employed by companies around the world. I am even more amazed by how little most companies tap into the innovative potential of these employees. This book provides dozens of proven tips and techniques that will enable you to get the most out of your workforce.

Innovation is the key to long-term growth. Although many companies are enamored with utilizing best practices, as this book's title suggests, duplicating what others are already doing relegates you to a continuous game of catch-up. Following in the footsteps of others is the fastest way to irrelevancy. Instead, create your own path. Find new and creative ways of staying ahead of the competition. Only through repeated, rapid, and efficient change can an organization survive and thrive in today's volatile marketplace.

> With most innovation strategies, finding a good idea is like finding a specific needle in a stack of other needles.

Innovate the Way You Innovate

Before diving into the specifics of the innovation capability, let's review some key innovation concepts. Not everyone will share my point of view in this section. That's expected, as these tips challenge the conventional wisdom that dominates popular thought. However, the high failure rate of most innovation efforts tells us that these conventional approaches may not be so wise after all. Ready? Let's get started.

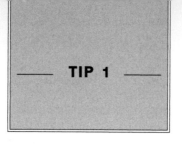

Not Survival of the Fittest— Survival of the Adaptable

Have you heard the one about two men who are hiking through the mountains of Canada? The story goes that after stumbling upon a hungry, six-hundred-pound grizzly bear, one of the hikers takes off his backpack and his hiking boots and proceeds to put on his running shoes. The other hiker looks at him and asks, "What are you doing? You can't outrun a bear!" The first hiker responds, "I know, but I only need to outrun you!"

This story highlights the essence of innovation. Innovation is not about new products, new processes, new services, new business models, or even new ideas. It is about staying one step ahead of your competition so that you are not eaten. Let's face it, there are a lot of hungry competitors out there. And when you are trying to outpace the bear (your current competition), you need to make sure you don't run into an alligator or a tiger (your new competition).

Innovation is about change. Not a onetime change but ongoing change. It is about adaptability, flexibility, and agility.

Consider this. . . .

When the pace of change outside your organization is greater than the pace of change within, you will be eaten and have a tough time keeping your business afloat. And as you know, the pace of change outside of your organization is faster than ever.

The *only* way to survive is to stop treating innovation as a onetime event. Innovation must be a continuous, never-ending process. The second you rest on your laurels, you can be certain that someone will catch you for breakfast.

But the story of the two hikers does not end with the first hiker saying, "I only need to outrun you." It continues with the second hiker saying, "Go ahead and try," and then standing perfectly still as the first hiker takes off. The second hiker smiles because he knows that bears have poor eyesight and will only chase prey that runs away. The first hiker gets eaten. The second hiker reflects on the importance of understanding the hunting habits of large carnivores—and of choosing friends wisely.

The moral of the story is that, although organizations want to speed up their innovation efforts and move quickly, running in the wrong direction can actually slow you down and burn valuable resources. Instead, take deliberate action. Know what will improve your business. Understand the marketplace and harness the energies of your organization by focusing on what is most important.

And yes, pick your friends—and colleagues—wisely. The people you choose as your innovation partners are an important part of your innovation strategy.

So what can an organization do to not get eaten by the competition?

THE THREE LEVELS OF INNOVATION

The answer to that lies in a basic understanding of the three levels of innovation.

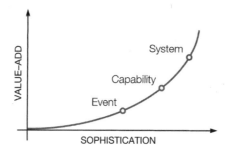

LEVEL 1: INNOVATION AS AN EVENT: This is where most companies find themselves. They conduct brainstorming sessions or hold random contests to generate new ideas. If a good idea is produced, there is some value added to the organization. In some cases, the idea may even lead to tremendous value (such as 3M's invention of Post-it notes). However, there is generally a huge amount of work that needs to happen between an idea's generation and its realization.

LEVEL 2: INNOVATION AS A CAPABILITY: This is the next level of sophistication. The organization puts in place structures and processes to define problems, generate and evaluate solutions, and develop action plans to implement those solutions. The result is a realistic deliverable based on an organizational challenge or opportunity.

LEVEL 3: INNOVATION AS A SYSTEM: The ultimate level involves creating an environment where innovation is embedded in everything you do. At both the event- and capability-driven levels, innovation tends to be reactionary and discrete. It is somewhat separate from the business. With embedded innovation, people innovate to deal not only with "problems or challenges" that are presented to them but with everything they do. They continuously, even radically, improve their products, processes, and organization. This creates exponential and ongoing value.

Where do you begin?

The first step is to create an environment where creativity is encouraged and where solutions are implemented in response to specific challenges. This is level 2: innovation as a repeatable process and capability. In fact, a large portion of this book is dedicated to helping organizations achieve that level. Once this is mastered, you can more easily move on to innovation as a system: the holy grail of innovation.

Too often, organizations send employees to creativity classes. When these individuals return, they are excited about generating new ideas. Unfortunately, they are confronted with an environment that stifles creativity and innovation. They are told to keep their heads down and their mouths shut. There is no vehicle for tapping into their new creative energies. They become disgruntled and frustrated. Now you have a bigger morale problem. Creative ideas without an encouraging innovation environment lead to employee dissatisfaction. An overall shift toward a culture of innovation must be put in place before people can be trained to be creative thinkers.

Although people believe that Darwin suggested that it is the survival of the fittest, his perspective on "natural selection" was that it is not physical shape but rather the ability to adapt that is critical.

This is the goal of innovation. The smartest organization will not survive. The company with the most money can quickly fall from grace. But the organization that adapts and evolves to address ever-changing market conditions will thrive in the long run.

> When the pace of change outside your organization is greater than the pace of change within, you will be eaten.

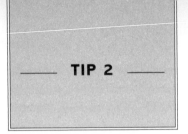

How Can You Avoid Becoming a One-Hit Wonder?

Do you know the bands Lipps, Inc., the Sugarhill Gang, or Haddaway? You might know the song that each of these artists made famous: "Funkytown," "Rapper's Delight," and "What Is Love," respectively. These artists were "one-hit wonders." They climbed to the top of the music charts once and were never heard from again.

This is not too dissimilar to what happens with many businesses. They generate one good idea to gain momentum but quickly fall from grace. What can you do to prevent your organization from becoming a one-hit wonder? Make sure that your innovation efforts are predictable and sustainable by treating them like any other capability in your company.

As an example, think about your organization's finance capability. It has skilled experts (e.g., CPAs), measures (e.g., days sales outstanding), supporting technology (e.g., Oracle or SAP), processes (e.g., one for closing the books at year-end), an owner (the CFO), and a strategy. Your innovation capability requires all of these elements and more, including skilled innovation experts, innovation measures, innovation management technologies, an innovation process, an innovation "owner," and a clearly articulated innovation strategy.

With these pieces in place, you can begin to make innovation a repeatable and predictable process where creativity is encouraged throughout the organization and the best solutions are implemented. This is the second level of innovation described in the previous tip: innovation as a capability.

Five key components are required for successful long-term innovation.

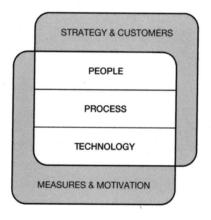

STRATEGY: A strategy is needed to decide when, where, and how innovation will be used within the organization. Most important, it should address why you want innovation. Are you looking primarily for a new pipeline of products? Do you want to serve your customers better? Are you looking to create a more nimble, flexible, and adaptable organization? For one company, the mantra for innovation was "2×10"—to become a two-billion-dollar business by 2010. This made it clear to all employees why innovation was needed and what it means to deliver innovative ideas. Another company is solely focused on its customers, with the mantra "Innovation is anything that makes the lives of our customers better."

MEASURES: Innovation, like any capability, needs to be measurable and measured. You will want to measure the value of your innovation pipeline. Who will be measured? What kinds of measures will be used? How will you measure less tangible values, such as adaptability? How will you relate innovation to overall business outcomes and results?

PEOPLE: Your people are your culture. If you want a culture of innovation, your employees must embrace actions, values, beliefs, skills, and language that are consistent with this objective. Everyone, at all levels, must appreciate divergent points of view. Creativity must be encouraged and valued. And you need the right organization and leadership models in place.

PROCESS: Innovation requires an end-to-end model for targeting, generating, selecting, and implementing innovative solutions. As you will discover, the recommended innovation process is one that starts with a challenge and ends with value created for the organization.

TECHNOLOGY: Innovative companies use collaboration tools to enable communication among employees, customers, suppliers, and external experts. Solutions are captured in ways that facilitate the dissemination and replication of innovative thinking. These technologies enable communication at all levels, across all organizations, and across business boundaries.

You will notice that this book is, for the most part, organized around each of these components, providing even greater detail on how to implement an innovation capability in your organization.

For too long, innovation has been relegated to the darkest recesses of research and development (R&D) departments and to the conference rooms of well-meaning brainstormers. But now is the time to bring innovation to the forefront of your business. Now is the time to make innovation a capability with the same level of status as finance, sales, or marketing. Doing this will prevent your innovation efforts from becoming a one-hit wonder.

> For too long, innovation has been relegated to the darkest recesses of R&D departments and to the conference rooms of well-meaning brainstormers. But now is the time to bring innovation to the forefront of your business.

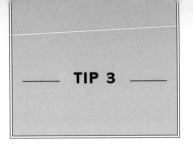

Asking for Ideas Is a Bad Idea

A large European retail bank that was suffering from eroding market share thought it had a great idea to solve this emerging problem. Its executives decided to get input from all of the employees on ways to improve and grow the business. In order to collect employee ideas, they implemented an enterprise-wide electronic suggestion box. They believed that this would help them tap into previously undiscovered innovations. Sounds like a great idea, right? Wrong!

They received thousands of ideas. Evaluators looked at every one, and in the end, none were implemented. The company's entire innovation program lasted a total of eighteen months, at which point it was shut down and deemed a huge failure.

In an attempt to be more innovative, many companies start by asking employees for their ideas. This is a bad idea! The ideas that are submitted tend to be impractical and of low value and end up only creating an overwhelming amount of unproductive clutter in the system.

This points to one of the most important yet underconsidered measures in the innovation process: the "signal-to-noise ratio."

The signal-to-noise ratio is an engineering term that is used to quantify how much a signal is corrupted by noise. For example, in an audio recording, the signal is the music and the noise is any background hiss. A higher ratio indicates more signal than noise, which is the ultimate goal. Many online discussion forums use the term to describe the ratio between useful information and spam or false/irrelevant information.

This latter use of the term is the one that best applies to innovation.

In innovation, the signal is composed of solutions that are implemented and create value. The noise is made up of all of the ideas that never come to fruition and the useless suggestions that don't matter and don't create value.

To increase your innovation's signal-to-noise ratio, the first thing you want to do is stop asking for ideas.

Suggestion boxes are cluttered with noise, and the amount of time required to sift through bad ideas to get to the gold is huge. Even when you do find a good suggestion, the amount of effort required to rally the troops to implement the idea can be significant.

In the aftermath of the bank's innovation efforts, I was asked to do a postmortem assessment of what went wrong. In going through the submissions, I found that the ideas could be categorized into three broad groups:

DUDS: A large percentage of the ideas were clearly not worth pursuing. They were not new or were unlikely to show a positive ROI. There might have been a nugget of usefulness among these suggestions that was missed. However, the energy required to nurture these nuggets was probably not worth the effort.

FALSE NEGATIVES: These were good ideas, but for whatever reason the evaluators dismissed them. Part of it had to do with the biases of the evaluators, and sometimes it was due to a lack of knowledge on their part. Oftentimes these ideas were dismissed because they were not fully developed, making it difficult for them to be properly judged.

GOOD IDEA, NO HOME: This was the most disconcerting category. These were good ideas that the evaluators liked, but sadly there was no organizational home or strategy for implementing them. As a result, the ideas withered on the vine and were never used. They never got the resources or funding necessary to move them to the next level.

The bank's experience is not unique among organizations. A well-known software company had an "idea program" that generated tens of thousands of suggestions. Fewer than a dozen proved to have any value, and the program was completely scrapped.

One large retailer is known for holding a well-publicized competition each year where employees (and in some cases customers) submit new product ideas. The winner gets a large check and the company implements the best idea. I asked the person responsible for this program if it was a success. He thought about it a moment and responded, "It was a PR success but a commercial failure." The competition generated buzz in the media, but none of the products ever generated a positive return on investment.

While the company's idea-based competitions did not generate good bottom-line results, its programs that focused on addressing specific product-improvement opportunities were a huge commercial success. The fact that this company recently stopped running its annual idea competition gives you a sense of how much value those innovative ideas brought to the company.

The other problem with asking for ideas is that there is no level of accountability. Because people tend to develop ideas on their own time, there are no tracking methods that can keep tabs on how much energy is invested in idea generation. If you encourage ideas, you are probably spending more money on those initiatives than you could ever imagine. You might be able to measure the ROI of a specific winning idea, but it is difficult to determine the ROI of your overall idea-based program. There is no way to know how much time was spent on the thousands of duds that never see the light of day.

My suggestion? Throw out your suggestion box!

Organizations are often enamored with collecting a large number of ideas from employees and customers. And although these can be useful for employee morale, if you go down this path, your organization needs to make sure to implement enough of the ideas to keep enthusiasm high. Unfortunately, the lack of traction gained by most idea platforms hurts morale and leaves the organization with a lot of extra work.

If you have an infinite amount of resources, time, and money, then the idea-driven approach can be useful for finding hidden gems.

But sometimes the best idea is to stop asking for ideas.

> One of the most important yet underconsidered measures in the innovation process is the signal-to-noise ratio.

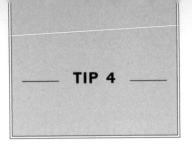

Don't Think Outside the Box;
Find a Better Box

Leaders of organizations often use the expression "Think outside the box" when urging their employees to innovate. The belief is that eliminating constraints and allowing people to think freely will increase creativity.

Although this tabula rasa, or "blank slate," method of innovation is conventional wisdom, this unbounded approach actually reduces creativity and leads to abstract or impractical solutions. A television scriptwriter in Hollywood once told me that he actually liked the idea of "creativity within constraints," as it gave him a starting point and then he could "riff" from there.

Instead of telling your employees to think outside the box, give them a "better box" to innovate inside of. These constraints will actually increase creativity and lead to useful solutions.

Albert Einstein reputedly said, "If I had an hour to save the world, I would spend fifty-nine minutes defining the problem and one minute finding solutions." In my experience, most companies spend the full sixty minutes finding solutions to problems that just don't matter.

Well-defined challenges guide innovation efforts, provide useful constraints, and define that "better box."

CHALLENGE-DRIVEN INNOVATION

All companies have challenges. They can be technical challenges on how to create a particular chemical compound. They can be marketing challenges on how to best describe your product to increase market share. They can be HR challenges around improving employee engagement. Or they can be process improvement challenges. Let's face it: Your organization has no shortage of problems and you can find these challenges everywhere—from your customers, employees, shareholders, consultants, vendors, competitors, and more.

An organization's ability to change (i.e., innovate) hinges on its ability to identify and solve these challenges.

WHY CHALLENGE-DRIVEN INNOVATION?

There are a number of inherent advantages to using a challenge-driven approach over an idea-driven approach to innovation:

- Challenges are the best way to ask your employees, customers, or any community for help. It allows them to focus their energies on finding solutions that will ultimately be relevant to the needs of the organization.
- Because of the nature of challenges, there are tools to evaluate the amount of time spent finding solutions. When challenge-

driven innovation is done properly, you can measure the ROI of each challenge and the overall program.

- With a challenge-driven approach, you can assign owners, resources and funding, evaluators, and evaluation criteria *before* investing the valuable time of employees and others.

  - *Owner/sponsor*—In nearly every situation, a challenge has a home; someone wants this problem solved. Therefore, assign the owner of the challenge up front. This ensures that when you get a solution, you can move things forward quickly.

  - *Resources and funding*—To implement any solution, you will need people and money. Given the importance and scope of a challenge, allocate these resources up front so that when a solution is found, you don't need to scramble.

  - *Evaluators*—When solutions are submitted, you will want a team of people to evaluate the submissions. Have evaluators in place who understand the big picture and will help ensure that the best solutions are selected.

  - *Evaluation criteria*—This one is important. Establish the evaluation criteria before posing the challenge, thereby creating a self-vetting process. This helps the people providing solutions know the boundaries that their solutions must meet, preventing fluffy or irrelevant answers.

The idea-driven approach to innovation does not allow for any of the above. With well-defined challenges, all of them are possible.

The difference between the idea-driven approach and the challenge-driven approach is analogous to the difference between two fishing techniques. Idea-driven approaches are like a fisherman choosing a random spot in the middle of the ocean and casting an extraordinarily expansive net. While using an untargeted approach like this might yield some fish, that fisherman will also collect shoes, tires, seaweed, and other undesirable items. And the fish he does catch will probably not be the specific type he was looking for.

Contrast that with a fisherman who purposefully locates a school of fish and then deliberately selects the appropriate rod, reel, line, leader, bait, and hook for catching exactly the type of fish he wants, effectively minimizing waste and maximizing the effect of his efforts. As the old expression goes: "If you want to catch fish, go where the fish are." This is the challenge-driven approach.

Establishing boundaries does not necessarily put constraints on innovation efforts. In actuality, if done correctly, it has the capacity to dramatically enhance creativity and increase organizational effectiveness. So the next time you are tempted to say, "Think outside the box," think again.

Albert Einstein once said, "If I had an hour to save the world, I would spend fifty-nine minutes defining the problem and one minute finding solutions." Unfortunately, most companies spend sixty minutes finding solutions to problems that just don't matter.

Expertise Is the Enemy of Innovation

Unilever, the giant consumer goods company, wanted to develop a toothpaste that would whiten teeth without using the traditional methods of bleach or abrasives. The toothpaste experts didn't have a solution. Recognizing the limitations of their own knowledge, they asked themselves, "Who makes whites whiter?" They quickly realized that a different Unilever business unit made laundry detergents that whitened clothes without bleach. What they learned was that most detergents use a blueing agent to make whites *appear* whiter. Armed with this information, they created their "Signal White Now" (and other brands) toothpaste. Instead of using harsh bleaches and abrasives, the toothpaste has a blue dye that runs through the middle and creates the immediate optical illusion of white teeth. Toothpaste experts were seemingly unable to solve this problem on their own. This breakthrough solution was discovered only when people with different specializations were brought together.

While this might seem surprising, it is not uncommon. Expertise can indeed be the enemy of breakthrough thinking. The more you know about a particular topic, the more difficult it is for you to think about it in a different way. Your solutions will most likely be "been there, done that" ideas that are limited to your area of expertise. If you want breakthroughs, you need to bring together people from a wide range of disciplines, backgrounds, and experiences.

This idea was confirmed by research completed by Lee Fleming, a business administration professor at Harvard Business School. By analyzing seventeen thousand patents, he discovered that the breakthroughs that arise from multidisciplinary work "are frequently of unusually high value—superior to the best innovations achieved by conventional approaches."

His research highlighted the pros and cons of each method. He learned that teams composed of people with similar backgrounds have a great number of successes yet yield fewer breakthroughs. On the other hand, cross-disciplinary teams have a higher failure rate, yet their innovations are more radical and have the potential to create incredible value.

Is there a way to get all of the benefits associated with diversity without any of the negative effects?

Yes. It is called open innovation.

Open innovation is an innovation process where you engage people outside your organization to help solve challenges. One common form of open innovation occurs when you post your challenges on a Web site and get responses from a diverse group of outside experts. Many organizations find that this is a useful tool for speeding up the innovation process because it taps into specializations that might not exist within the organization.

A widely publicized open innovation competition was the Netflix Prize. Netflix wanted to improve the quality of its video recommendation engine by 10 percent. This was valued as being worth millions of dollars in additional revenue. Instead of trying to improve the algorithm in house, the company decided to award one million dollars to the first person or team who could find a good solution. Although it took three years, a seven-person team of "statisticians, machine-learning experts, and computer engineers" from the United States, Austria, Canada, and Israel developed an algorithm that improved recommendations by 10.06 percent, resulting in their being awarded the prize money. For Netflix, this was a bargain. It would have cost the company much more to develop the solution internally, and who knows if it would have found one?

Here's how it works: You post a challenge to your Web site or the Web site of an intermediary. After a short period of time, you will receive dozens to hundreds of solutions, although a lot fewer than you would receive using idea-driven innovation. Although some won't be useful, all you need is one solution that does work. And with some forms of open innovation, you only pay for the solutions that do work. But the real advantage is that people from many disciplines can chime in with a variety of solutions, increasing the likelihood of a breakthrough. And if you do open innovation correctly, you won't be overloaded with useless submissions.

Remember the BP oil spill that was discussed earlier? BP received 123,000 ideas for solutions. Contrast that with the way open innovation was applied to another oil spill—the *Exxon Valdez* disaster.

Back in 1989 the *Exxon Valdez* tanker crashed into a reef in Prince William Sound in Alaska, dumping 10.8 million gallons of crude oil into the water. Although some of the oil was recovered, a large amount remained trapped under the ice. When teams tried to move the oil, the water/oil mixture froze. Oil engineers worked on this challenge for twenty years without any viable solution until they discovered open innovation. They posted a well-formed challenge to the Web site of an intermediary, InnoCentive, a company that has a large network of experts from a wide range of disciplines who solve complex problems for monetary prizes.

A solution to the oil crisis was found very quickly. Interestingly, the winning solution did not come from the oil industry. Instead, it came from someone in the construction industry who had a similar challenge with pouring wet cement; he needed to find a way of preventing it from hardening right away. This chemist developed a device that vibrates the molecules so that they flow continuously. He figured that if vibrations could keep cement from hardening, then a similar concept could be adapted to keep the oil in the tanks from freezing. Bringing together diverse disciplines through an open innovation platform solved this decades-old problem.

Another great example comes from NASA. Solar activity is a major problem for space travel and can be incredibly dangerous for astronauts. For decades, NASA scientists had been unsuccessful in trying to find a model that would allow them to predict solar activity with a high level of accuracy.

To find a solution, they turned to open innovation. Their success criteria for the solution were that the model should provide a prediction within twenty-four hours of the solar activity, be 50 percent accurate, and be within two sigma (a quality measure where higher numbers are better). The best solution predicted activity within eight hours, was 70 percent accurate, and was within three sigma. This was a huge improvement over NASA's initial expectations. Who had the solution? A retired engineer who studied dropped cell phone calls and in the process had discovered a predictive model for solar flares.

Sometimes the best solutions come from outside your area of expertise and beyond the four walls of your organization. In the end, you might just find solutions to problems that have stumped the experts for years.

If you are NASA and you have 100 aerospace engineers working on an aerospace engineering challenge, adding the 101st aerospace engineer may not help that much. But adding a physicist, a nanotechnologist, a chemist, a biologist, or even a musician may move your solutions in a completely new direction.

Challenge-Driven Innovation

Efficient innovation requires an efficient innovation process. When done correctly, the innovation process starts with a challenge and ends with value creation. Unfortunately, the process used by most organizations is unfocused and actually creates unnecessary work. This section explores various aspects of the innovation process: challenges, competition, collaboration, and crowdsourcing. Your innovation efforts will be more focused and efficient if you use a combination of these strategies.

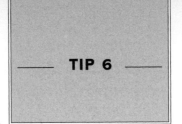

TIP 6

The Difference Between a Pipeline and a Sewer Is What Flows Through It

We hear the expression "innovation pipeline" tossed around a lot. But if you aren't careful, your pipeline may get clogged.

The biggest challenge companies face is figuring out which challenges to solve. I call this their "meta-challenge." Given that organizations have limited resources and money, prioritization is critical.

Several well-known companies have invested poorly in innovation, resulting in disaster. Although Blockbuster Inc., the national video rental chain, was constantly innovating, it was never innovating where it needed to most: its business model. As a result, it invested a lot of energy, yet went nowhere quickly, eventually landing in bankruptcy. Likewise, Xerox's fabled Palo Alto Research Center (PARC) was always focused on radical and game-changing innovations, yet it never found ways to bring its inventions to market. Apple was the ultimate beneficiary of PARC's hard work.

You want to manage your innovation pipeline the way you manage your personal investment portfolio. Putting all of your money in a savings account making 1 percent interest may be safe, but your investment will never grow and you will most likely end up destitute. Then again, putting all of your money in risky derivatives and speculative investments that have a large potential upside has an equally large downside and will most likely land you in the gutter. The buzzword in the finance world is "diversification."

YOUR INNOVATION PORTFOLIO

Equally, your innovation portfolio should be composed of a diverse set of investments in various types of challenges. Include some safe bets (incremental innovation) along with some riskier investments (radical innovation). It's up to you to decide the correct proportion. You want a variety of challenges, ranging from service to product-enhancement challenges and performance-improvement to business-model-changing challenges.

Challenges tend to fall into two broad categories: technical challenges (e.g., how do we create a new chemical compound with specific properties?) and marketing challenges (e.g., how do we get women to drink more beer?).

When you map these two dimensions, you get the following chart with four broad categories of challenges (at the top of next page).

INCREMENTAL INNOVATION: This is the portfolio equivalent of investing in CDs and money markets. These are safe and yield returns. This is where the lion's share of innovation money is invested, as it should be. But don't put all of your eggs in this

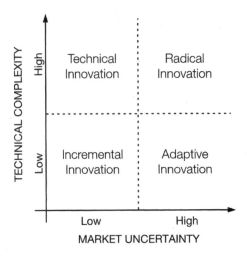

basket. Too many safe bets, in the long run, are unsafe. Generally, these innovations are both technically easy and have a clear customer benefit. The next generation of your product or service, for example, would often fall into this category.

ADAPTIVE INNOVATION: These are challenges that are easy to implement from a technical perspective but represent a departure from a known market need. As a result, you don't know if consumers will be interested or how to get them interested. For example, when Chrysler introduced the minivan, it was an incremental technical effort but presented a complex marketing challenge, since nothing like it had previously existed. In other cases, the innovation is about adapting an old product and bringing it to a new market. For example, a razor blade company wanted to find ways to get teenage boys to shave more often. For these challenges, experimentation combined with sophisticated market research is often the answer. (See tips 13, 14, and 24.)

TECHNICAL INNOVATION: This category deals with any innovation that serves a well-established need yet is technically complex to develop. The obvious example is finding a better cure for a disease, but other examples might include NASA's need for predictive modeling of solar flare activity or creating a razor blade made of plastic with the strength of steel. For these types of challenges, as you will discover, open innovation (described in the previous tip) is an extremely useful technique for finding solutions to technically complex challenges. (See tips 8 through 11.)

RADICAL INNOVATION: These innovations are both technically complex and have a high level of market uncertainty. The Sony Walkman (now retired) is a well-worn example of this. Apple's integration of iTunes with the iPod could fall into this category, as the "technically" difficult part was getting all of the artists and recording studios to agree to allow digital music to be sold. These challenges are the riskiest, as they can be costly with a lower likelihood of success. But when successful, these innovations can be game changing.

It is not important to debate where specific challenges might fall. For example, you could argue that the iPod/iTunes met a known market need, since consumers were already downloading digital music from Napster, albeit without paying. The key is to make sure that you have a good balance of the different types of challenges. This can help you hedge your bets.

In Lewis Carroll's *Through the Looking-Glass*, the Red Queen says, "It takes all the running you can do, to keep in the same place." Investing only in incremental innovation results in a lot of hard work with little progress. On the other hand, always swinging for the fences will have you striking out most of the time. Diversify your innovation portfolio and you will keep your pipeline flowing smoothly.

> Too many safe bets, in the long run, are unsafe.

TIP 7

The Goldilocks Principle

Remember the story of Goldilocks? She enters the house of three bears. After sampling their porridge, she decides to go to sleep. She finds the papa bear's bed too hard, the mama bear's bed too soft, and the baby bear's bed just right. The same is true when defining challenges. They can't be too big (broad and abstract, e.g., asking for "new ideas") or too small (overly specific, e.g., an extremely technical problem that can be solved only by one discipline). They must be "just right"—framed in a way that maximizes the likelihood of finding a workable solution.

When framing challenges, you must adhere to the Goldilocks Principle.

> **TOO BIG**
> Broad and Abstract

> **JUST RIGHT**
> Maximum Likelihood
> of Being Solved

> **TOO SMALL**
> Overly Specific
> and Single Discipline

It is quite common for a company to ask its employees to find ways to increase revenue. This is a lofty goal, and posing this type of general challenge usually results in fluffy solutions. Instead of asking people to solve broad problems, ask specific questions that will likely result in an implementable solution. For example, are there specific markets that you have not yet penetrated? Are you missing out on customer segments that present a greater opportunity?

When a cell phone company wanted to improve customer service, instead of simply asking people how to improve the customer experience, the company analyzed call data and found that there were ten primary reasons why people dialed in to the call center. One of the most common reasons had to do with a specific billing issue. The solution? It was concluded that the best way to improve customer service in the call center had nothing to do with the call center itself. Instead, it involved a change in the tariffs associated with this particular issue. This one small change resulted in dramatically reduced call volumes and higher customer satisfaction. The only way that this solution could have been found was by asking a more specific question backed up by data.

Or consider a not-for-profit organization that wanted to improve the educational system of England. Another lofty goal indeed, and had the organization's leaders asked people for solutions to such a large problem, the answers would have been all over the map. Instead, they did their research. They discovered that the greatest factor in a child's education was not the educational system itself but rather parental involvement. Therefore, the challenge became how to increase parental involvement in a child's education, particularly in urban, disadvantaged communities. The data and research they had collected provided deeper insights. The solutions were more focused, practical, and valuable than they would have been had the question been more generally focused on the entire educational system. The winning solution was based on work done at an experimental school in Bogotá, Colombia, where parental involvement reached nearly 100 percent and student learning skyrocketed. A solution found halfway around the world now had the potential to change the educational outcomes of students in the UK.

NASA has had great success with open innovation. Its scientists have found solutions to problems that have plagued space travel for decades. One challenge was designed to find a "microgravity laundry system." The solutions they received were not as useful as they had hoped. In hindsight, they recognized two important lessons.

First, they realized that a "system" question might have been too complex, and the larger challenge might have been more effectively solved if it had been deconstructed into a series of smaller challenges (e.g., a valve challenge).

The second and potentially more important lesson was that they might have been better served by asking an even higher-level question. That is, asking about a laundry system implied that the solution was mechanical in nature. However, they might have found more interesting solutions had they asked about how to eliminate the need for clothes laundering altogether. This might have led to a completely different breakthrough. So in this case, you could argue that the original challenge was too narrowly defined.

The previously discussed *Exxon Valdez* oil spill provides another example of a challenge being initially too narrowly defined. When the "freezing" problem was posed as an oil challenge, only oil experts worked on the problem. When the challenge was posed as a "viscous shearing" issue, the problem was no longer about oil (a specific fluid) but rather about a common problem in fluid dynamics. When the challenge was phrased this way, it allowed for solutions from a broad range of disciplines, including the construction industry, where the fix was eventually found.

A critical step in trying to find solutions is to clearly define the challenge. The way a challenge is framed will impact the way it is solved.

Some might suggest that Goldilocks's decision to enter the home belonging to the three bears in the woods was not very sound. However, it was her quest for "just right" that allowed her to rest peacefully. If you adopt this same rigor when defining your challenges, you too might sleep a bit better at night knowing a workable solution is just around the corner.

Challenges can't be too big (broad and abstract, e.g., asking for "new ideas") or too small (overly specific, e.g., an extremely technical problem that can be solved only by one discipline). They must be "just right"—framed in a way that maximizes the likelihood of finding a workable solution.

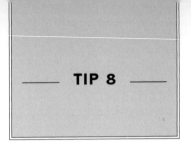

There Is No Such Thing as a "Know-It-All"

Recently, a well-known health-care company was faced with a tricky challenge. After launching an incredibly successful new product, it turned its attention to creating new complementary offerings. Multiple failed attempts later, it came to realize that it didn't have the in-house expertise to crack the problem. Not knowing what to do, executives decided to try posting the challenge on an open innovation Web site. Their hope was that they could find someone outside their organization who could find a practical solution.

Unfortunately, some employees took this action as a slap in the face. Unfamiliar with the benefits of open innovation, they felt that someone within the organization could solve every challenge. To prove their point, several employees took it upon themselves to submit solutions to the posted challenge.

In the end, the solutions submitted by the employees weren't chosen. The breakthrough answer came from someone not only outside the company but outside the company's industry. The successful conclusion of this challenge solidified the executives' decision to formally launch the company's open innovation efforts. Their conclusion?

No one person can solve every problem.

And its corollary: No one organization can solve every problem.

The late, great Will Rogers once said, "There is nothing so stupid as an educated man, if you get him off the thing that he was educated in."

One of the challenges of driving innovation in organizations is that smart people are often more interested in being right than in doing right. That is, they want to believe that they can solve every problem under the sun. This pervasive belief can thwart your innovation efforts.

To be clear, the objective of open innovation is not to replace the smarts you already have in your organization. It is to augment this brilliance. Most companies don't have enough time to solve all of the challenges they are working on. Unfortunately, R&D people often get spread too thin working on a lot of different types of challenges, some of which could be better solved by others outside the company.

Here's a simple model I use to help companies determine which challenges should be solved externally and which can be solved internally.

Broadly speaking, challenges fall into three categories. (See graphic at the top of the next page.)

SIMPLE CHALLENGES: On the left-hand side of the bell curve, you have the challenges where there is a high probability that someone else has already solved this specific problem. Although you

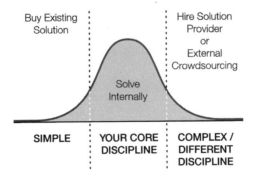

could solve them internally, this is not the best use of your resources. The odds are that someone else already has a solution that you could buy or license for less money in less time. Why waste your highly specialized experts on these types of challenges?

- *Buying an Existing Solution:* For these types of challenges, tech scouting (as an example) is a great way to procure existing solutions by scanning patent databases and other technology repositories. You can then license or purchase the technology for your own use. With this strategy you are buying a solution from a single provider.

COMPLEX OR UNSOLVED CHALLENGES: On the right-hand side of the bell curve, you have the challenges that are exceptionally complex and may have remained unsolved within your organization for years. Or maybe they are things that are viewed as being outside your area of expertise. For example, because space travel can last for years, NASA had a problem with food spoilage. Over the years, it had tried different packaging material with no success. Even people from the food packaging industry could not find a solution. With nowhere else to turn, NASA decided to run an open innovation challenge. The solution it found came from someone in Russia with no food experience. He developed a graphite-based material that appears to keep food fresher longer than regular materials.

In general, for these types of complex challenges, there are two primary strategies for finding solutions: (1) hiring a solution provider or (2) crowdsourcing a solution.

- *Hiring a Solution Provider:* With this strategy, a third party takes ownership of delivering the result and can solve some challenges (and potentially implement the solutions). You might choose to work with a university or you might issue a "request for proposal" in order to find a solution provider. Regardless, in these situations, you aren't buying a solution as much as you're selecting an outsourcing partner. These alliances are best used for complex challenges that can't be deconstructed into smaller ones or where deep context knowledge is required.
- *Crowdsourcing a Solution:* Posting your problem to "the world" and allowing a few weeks or months for someone to submit a workable solution is the best way to solve other challenges. Then you can buy or license the solution. The difference between this and the previous approach is that here you are buying a solution, not a solution provider. Crowdsourcing is great for technically complex challenges

that can be defined at a right level of granularity, like the NASA food spoilage challenge.

CHALLENGES WITHIN YOUR DISCIPLINE: In the middle of the bell curve are the challenges that fall into the sweet spot of your organization. These are the challenges that your experts are best equipped to solve. By outsourcing the simple and complex/unsolved challenges, you can allow your team to focus on what they do best. This will increase your ability to solve the problems that differentiate you from your competition. Although there are several methods for finding solutions internally, here are the two most common approaches:

- *Internal Individual/Team:* This is the most common way challenges are solved. You use internal people whose job it is to solve these types of challenges. For example, this would include members of the development team assigned to a particular product. The solutions may come from brainstorming or through a deep technical understanding of the problem. This method is the preferred approach when a deep contextual understanding is required and would be difficult to transfer elsewhere. It is obviously a good place to start for solving many types of challenges.
- *Internal Crowdsourcing:* Sometimes people inside your organization who are not already assigned to the given problem find the best solutions. It might be a customer service representative who finds a great new branding solution or a researcher located in a different part of the organization who solves a technical challenge. These

solutions are typically found by posting the challenge on your intranet or on a platform specifically designed for this purpose. This is typically a good place to turn next when the dedicated team can't find an answer. (See appendix A for information on crowdsourcing tools.)

As they say, there is more than one way to skin a cat. And there is definitely more than one way to solve a challenge. Although some challenges are solved in a moment of genius, most require a more formal thought process. The key to efficient innovation is determining which mechanism would best yield a viable solution for that specific challenge.

The approaches listed above represent only a few of the possible strategies. If one technique (e.g., internal team) does not yield a workable solution, try a different approach (e.g., external crowdsourcing). People want to be (and should be) appreciated for their brilliance. They have dedicated their lives to the pursuit of knowledge. But everyone cannot be educated in everything. Figure out what you (and your organization) do best, and find others to help with everything else.

Or, to quote Will Rogers again, "Everybody is ignorant. Only on different subjects."

"There is nothing so stupid as an educated man, if you get him off the thing that he was educated in." —Will Rogers

TIP 9

What Did Edison Get Wrong About Innovation?

While attempting to find a suitable filament to make the incandescent electric light a viable device, Edison is famous for saying, "I have not failed seven hundred times. I have not failed once. I have succeeded in proving that those seven hundred ways will not work. When I have eliminated the ways that will not work, I will find the way that will work."

Depending on the source, Edison tried seven hundred, one thousand, or ten thousand different filaments in his attempt to improve the lightbulb.

Regardless of which number is accurate, innovators around the world continue to embrace this quote because it seems to validate the iterative development process used by so many. There is a widely held belief that you should keep on trying and failing until you find a solution that works, because you learn as much from failure as you do from success.

Regardless, each of Edison's seven hundred attempts cost him time and money.

If Edison had found a solution to the lightbulb challenge on the first try, would he have continued to seek out seven hundred other ways that did not work? Did finding ways that did not work really add that much value? Can your organization afford seven hundred unsuccessful attempts? Not in today's competitive environment.

Think about it this way. . . .

ITERATIVE DEVELOPMENT

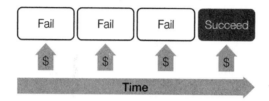

Look at the chart above. With the traditional model you fail over and over again until you are finally successful. Because your employees are working and investing their time on each attempt, it costs the organization payroll and overhead. And because the failure process happens serially, it takes a long time. Of course, if you are successful on the first attempt, life is good. But that rarely happens in the real world.

Unfortunately, the reality is that failure is often a necessary part of innovation. We can never instantly know the solution to a problem until we test it out via experimentation (see tip 24). But is there a better way to find solutions that minimize your risk, cost, and time—especially for technical challenges?

The chart at the top of the next page is based on a challenge-driven, open innovation model. Alph Bingham, founder of

MASSIVE PARALLEL PROCESS

InnoCentive, describes challenge-driven open innovation as a "massively parallel process where failures and successes happen at the same time." With this approach, you have the same number of failures, but there are two differences. One: The failures are happening in parallel rather than in a series, significantly speeding up your time to solution. Two: The cost of failure is pushed into the market and you pay only for value received, instead of paying for the time invested. That is, you pay only for a successful solution.

Say you post a challenge and you get dozens (or hundreds) of people working to find solutions. Some solutions won't work, but all you need is one that does work, and with this form of open innovation, you pay only for successful outcomes. Failures cost you nothing in terms of time and money. With internal iterative development, you pay for the successes and the failures.

Do you really learn enough from your failures to justify the extra cost and time involved? Probably not.

What should you do in order to take advantage of this massive parallel process?

For technically complex challenges (as opposed to challenges with market uncertainty, which are typically best tackled via experimentation), find ways of avoiding internal experimentation and identify others who can share the risk. Look for developers who are willing to be paid based on results rather than on time invested. The objective is to move away from the fixed costs associated with your internal development efforts and move toward a variable model where you pay only for the value of the solutions you need.

Edison was a great inventor. And I suspect that if Edison were alive today, given the tools available, he might try an entirely different approach to developing the sustainable filament.

Challenge-driven, open innovation is a "massively parallel process where failures and successes happen at the same time."
—Alph Bingham

What Do Cisco, LG Electronics, and GE Have in Common with *American Idol*?

American Idol, even after all these years, remains one of the most popular television shows. Why? Partly because it is entertaining and partly because the show is able to uncover previously undiscovered talent.

It is this latter reason why many organizations are employing the *American Idol* approach to innovation. Their objective is to uncover some truly amazing ideas or solutions that were previously hidden.

INNOVATION TOURNAMENTS

In the innovation space, these events are sometimes referred to as "innovation tournaments," a term coined by Christian Terwiesch and Karl Ulrich from the Wharton school in their book *Innovation Tournaments.*

The NCAA basketball championships are a tournament. The World Series of Poker is a tournament. Television's *Survivor, The Amazing Race,* and *Big Brother* are all tournaments. What makes each of these a tournament? Quite simply, there is always a winner, although it is not necessarily winner take all.

Cisco, LG Electronics, and GE have all used the "find a winner" model as a way to develop ideas.

The Cisco I-Prize was a tournament the company ran in 2010. When it was announced, Cisco said that it would "select up to 32 semifinalist teams that will work with Cisco experts to build a business plan and presentation. . . . Up to eight finalist teams will present their business ideas to a judging panel to compete for the grand prize: a $250,000 award shared equally by members of the winning team." In the end there were a total of 2,900 participants who submitted 824 ideas. Ideas were, as planned, narrowed down to thirty-two semifinalist ideas, with nine teams reaching the final phase of the tournament. The winning team did indeed receive $250,000.

LG Electronics held similar tournaments in 2009 and 2010. It was looking for people to "design their version of the next revolutionary LG mobile phone." A total of more than eighty thousand dollars in awards was given out, with the winner receiving twenty thousand dollars. The tournament had 835 submissions from 324 individuals. The company shared with me the fact that about 75 percent of the ideas were things it had thought of in the past; only 25 percent had innovative elements. The process was similar to the Cisco I-Prize approach: Judges reviewed all eight hundred plus concepts and narrowed them down to the top one hundred for round-two judges to review. Round-three judges only reviewed the top forty-three concepts.

GE is currently using a similar approach for its "ecomagination" challenges.

The common link among these tournaments is that there was always going to be a winner. Just as in *American Idol* and other tournaments, once they got through the duds, each organization had semifinalists, finalists, and the ultimate winner. But just because someone "wins" does not mean their talent or idea is good or even useful.

BOUNTY HUNTING

When is an innovation tournament not a tournament? And when is a tournament not the right approach?

When you are interested not in simply finding the "best" submission but rather in finding the "right" solution. That is, you don't want to crown a winner for the sake of naming a champion. Instead, the objective is to find workable solutions to a real and specific business problem.

Think of these as contingency-based, value-priced challenges. Admittedly, that does not sound as sexy as "innovation tournament."

Here's how it works: A company has a problem it wants solved. It decides the "value" of finding a workable solution and offers a "bounty" to anyone who can provide one. The bounty is paid only when the company gets what it needs. This "pay for solution" model outsources the risk associated with complex problem solving.

The two most well-known approaches to innovation bounties have been the Netflix Prize and the X Prize.

In the case of the Netflix Prize (described in tip 5), the company paid only the team that ultimately improved the recommendation engine by 10 percent. Netflix wasn't looking for the best solution; it was looking for one that met its specific needs. The bounty-based approach was useful because the company only paid the one million dollars when it received a successful solution.

The Ansari X Prize was a space competition in which twenty-six teams competed for a ten-million-dollar prize, which would be awarded to the first nongovernment organization to "build and launch a spacecraft capable of carrying three people to 100 kilometers above the Earth's surface, twice within two weeks." Just as with the Netflix Prize, the bounty was paid out only when the X Prize's specific criteria were met. Interestingly, although ten million dollars was awarded to the winning Tier One project's space plane, *SpaceShipOne*, it is reported that more than one hundred million dollars was invested in new technologies in pursuit of the prize.

TOURNAMENT VERSUS BOUNTY

The key difference is the way in which these challenges were articulated. With the bounty-based approach, the success criteria are clearly defined: Did you improve the recommendation engine by 10 percent? Did you find a chemical compound that has specific properties? Did you develop a mathematical model that optimizes a specific problem? The "winner" of the bounty is determined by the given criteria. If the criteria are not met, the bounty is not paid.

With the tournament-based approach, the success criteria are often not well defined. The winner is the "best" of the submissions. Although these types of competitions can yield excellent solutions, I know from inside information that the results are often less than stellar.

Tournaments are great for getting a broad set of ideas in an undefined space. And they are extremely useful for things, like the Pepsi Refresh Project, that are designed to generate a lot of buzz. Bounties, on the other hand, are great for when you are hunting down practical solutions. Use these when you want the best solution, not just the best of the bunch. However, both approaches can provide value to any organization when used in the right way.

> With the bounty-based approach, the success criteria are clearly defined. With the tournament-based approach, the winner is the "best" of the submissions.

TIP 11

To Compete or Not to Compete: That Is the Question

Open-source software is a well-known collaborative community. Many developers participate solely in order to be part of the community, to contribute to the greater good, and to build on one another's solutions. On the other hand, developers who work on creating apps for the iPhone operate in a competitive marketplace. Their contribution is largely, although not always, driven by financial return, and they tend to work independently.

Innovation tournaments and bounties (see previous tip) can be run either competitively or collaboratively. Cisco and LG Electronics ran competitive tournaments so that no one could see the rival submissions. GE, on the other hand, ran its eco-magination challenges collaboratively, allowing anyone to comment on or vote for any submission. The Netflix Prize and X Prize (both innovation bounties) were run as competitions yet allowed for collaboration within each submission.

This raises an important question. Which approach yields better solutions: competition or collaboration?

Kevin Boudreau and Karim Lakhani wrote an article on this topic in the *MIT Sloane Management Review* that examined the merits of each form of open innovation. They found that collaboration is useful when problems require "cumulative knowledge" and involve "building on past advances." On the other hand, competition is most effective when "an innovation problem is solved by broad experimentation."

They also found that collaborative "communities often are more oriented toward the intrinsic motivations of external innovators, whereas (competitive) markets tend to reward extrinsic motivation."

For your corporate innovation efforts, should you use competition or collaboration?

The answer is that you should use both. In fact, you may want to use both approaches for a single challenge. However, it is important to go about this in the right sequence.

Let's first address a few psychological issues related to creative thinking in humans.

Think about your typical group brainstorming session. Although this is a common way for organizations to innovate, is this approach effective? Interestingly, research suggests that individuals working on their own actually produce a higher quality and quantity of ideas than when they work collaboratively with others. There are several reasons for this:

- *Serial Processing:* If you have ten individuals in a group, only one can speak at any given time. This limits the "bandwidth" of ideas that can be processed. Ten people working individually could theoretically generate ten times more ideas in the same amount of time. However, using collaboration tools can eliminate this problem, as people can work in unison, allowing everyone to "speak" at the same time. IBM's Jam events are a popular way to get groups of people creating concurrently.

- *Social Loafing:* When groups work together, there is a tendency for individuals to put forth less effort. They assume that someone else will pick up the slack. Although this is true for group brainstorming sessions, when using other forms of innovation (such as open innovation), this factor tends to have a reduced impact.

- *Groupthink:* Finally, it has been shown that if you start the process by working together, you end up with groupthink. That is, as soon as the first idea is thrown out, it tends to influence the thinking of the other contributors. This causes a convergence of solutions too early in the process and narrows the set of ideas that are typically generated.

It is this last reason why it is good to start the process—whether you are using face-to-face brainstorming or virtual crowdsourcing—through a "competitive" approach to problem solving. When conducting brainstorming sessions, it works best to have each person independently write down his or her own creative ideas. Only after everyone generates their own list does the group come together. When using a crowdsourcing approach, it is often useful to start with a competition to get the widest range of solutions and then, only after selecting the best solutions, allow a collaborative community to flesh them out. This gives you a much richer solution in the end.

Several years ago I wanted a new logo for my Web site and decided to crowdsource a design using 99designs.com. After posting a "brief" describing what I wanted, I had a choice: Use a collaborative or a competitive approach. With the collaborative model, every designer could see the submissions of the other contributors, along with my comments on the designs. With the competitive approach, I could use blind submissions where the designers couldn't see anyone else's work. I chose the collaborative design approach. In the beginning, the designs trickled in slowly; many designers sat back and waited until there seemed to be a convergence around one idea. The variety of designs was relatively low.

I used a different approach when it came time to design the cards for my third book, *Personality Poker*. I first used the competitive model (i.e., blind submissions). I got a much greater variety of submissions right from the start, but there was no opportunity for people to build on the ideas of others. Therefore, after running the competition, I followed it up with a collaborative challenge. This process yielded a wide choice of initial designs followed by a high level of collaborative refinement. The final result was better than anything a single designer could have developed.

The most successful model, from this experience, was competition followed by collaboration.

Of course, there are other factors that will influence when you should use a competitive or a collaborative approach. For example, if intellectual property issues are critical, blind competitions work better since they provide greater protection for the designers. Of course, even in that situation, you can have groups work together to submit a competitive solution. When allocating prizes (monetary or other), competitions are easier to manage, as submissions are clearly delineated. But even with collaborative solutions, there are creative ways of divvying up the winnings. It does not need to be winner take all.

For social issues pertaining to the public good, collaboration often works well because you can take the pulse of a variety of people. Just don't fall into the trap of believing that public opinion will lead you to the right solution (see the next tip).

Every situation is different, and it is up to you to figure out which approach will work best for your particular challenge.

Collaboration and competition both serve an important purpose in the innovation process. As Alexander Graham Bell once said, "Great discoveries and improvements invariably involve the co-operation of many minds. I may be given credit for having blazed the trail, but when I look at the subsequent developments I feel the credit is due to others rather than to myself."

TIP 12

Crowds Are Better at Eliminating Duds Than at Picking Winners

Imagine you are the former governor of California, Arnold Schwarzenegger. Your state is struggling with a myriad of issues ranging from a perpetual and growing deficit to a decaying education system to an infrastructure that can't handle the ever-increasing population.

What do you do?

Like any good innovator, you turn to crowdsourcing, just as Governor Schwarzenegger did. He put up a Twitter-based site called MyIdea4CA.com, designed to allow anyone to post their suggestions and comments and vote on the best ideas. Thousands of people participated. Which idea (at one time) received the greatest support?

Did it involve reducing government spending? Did it help improve traffic and other infrastructure issues? Did it tackle educational issues? No. The winning idea was . . .

Legalize and tax marijuana.

Although the crowd felt that this might be the best way to solve many of the state's woes, it didn't solve any of the problems that the government wanted to handle.

In August 2009, a *New York Times* story detailed a similar effort by President Barack Obama to elicit ideas from the American public: "The White House made its first major entree into government by the people last month when it set up an online forum to ask ordinary people for their ideas on how to carry out the president's open-government pledge. It got an earful—on legalizing marijuana, revealing UFO secrets and verifying Mr. Obama's birth certificate to prove he was really born in the United States and thus eligible to be president."

Asking people for their opinions and allowing them to vote is not always the best way to run your innovation efforts.

What can we learn from all of this?

First and foremost, as stated in a previous tip, it is critical to clearly define the challenge. Both of these platforms were built around broad and ambiguous questions. Also, because of its Twitter-based platform, the MyIdea4CA site allowed only submissions that were fewer than 140 characters. It's hard to get into a meaty discussion, let alone provide deep and thoughtful solutions, in such a limited space.

But there is another important lesson here.

Crowdsourcing is not intended to be a democratic tool designed to gather the whims and wishes of individuals. It is intended to source solutions, not opinions.

Some might refer to what we are seeing on these sites as mobsourcing. This occurs when a few people lead the pack and provide most of the input, while the rest of the crowd hops on the bandwagon without adding anything meaningful to the discussion.

This explains why voting is not usually the most effective

way of sorting through ideas, suggestions, or solutions. Have you ever tried using a democratic voting mechanism as a means of whittling down a long list of submissions? If so, how effective was it? I suspect that it probably didn't work out as nicely as you had hoped. There are four primary reasons for this:

- Most voting systems are biased toward the solutions that were submitted the earliest. Early submissions get seen more often in the beginning and therefore get more votes. As a result, they become popular early on and continue to gain popularity. Think about this in the context of YouTube. A fantastic video that has one hundred views today may not get seen very often. But the video of a mouse riding a bicycle that has four million views today will probably have six million views by next week. Popularity begets popularity. There are more sophisticated "randomized" voting systems that exist to avoid this problem, ensuring that every entry gets seen by the same number of voters. But these approaches are not widely used and are effective only when you have a large number of voters who are willing to a look at a large number of submissions.

- Unless the submissions are anonymous—and they rarely are—people will naturally vote for the solutions submitted by their friends. In many organizations, people lobby for their solutions to receive votes. It becomes a popularity contest where individuals vote for the person and not the solution. This is not necessarily bad. If someone has taken the time to rally the troops to support their idea, that is a good

indicator of the submitter's enthusiasm, suggesting their idea might have a higher likelihood of success.

- People vote for self-serving solutions or ideas. This problem is exacerbated when using a suggestion-box approach instead of a challenge-driven approach. People will naturally vote for ideas that make *their* life better. It is human nature for self-interest to trump organizational needs.

- Most employees do not look at the big picture. Again, this is a larger problem with idea platforms than with challenge platforms. When down in the weeds, employees sometimes fail to see what is really needed and look only for solutions to things that are in their own peripheral vision. Unfortunately, these perspectives are not necessarily linked to customer needs or the company's overall strategic road map.

In general, what we find is that crowds are better at eliminating the duds than they are at picking the winners. Therefore, a potentially effective method is to use crowds to kill the really bad ideas so that experts can then review the few remaining plausible solutions. If you can eliminate 90 percent of the chaff using this method, you can radically speed up your review times. There are some more sophisticated methods (e.g., evaluating the standard deviation of rankings by the crowd to avoid false negatives), but these are more complicated and add only incremental value.

Although we often hear about the "wisdom of crowds," in reality, personal prejudices tend to bias the process. When crowdsourcing focuses on "how something should be done"

(solutions) rather than "what should be done" (voting), we are able to more effectively tap into the true intelligence of the masses.

> Crowdsourcing is not intended to be a democratic tool designed to gather the whims and wishes of individuals. It is intended to source solutions, not opinions.

Innovation Strategy and Customers

Customers must be at the heart of your innovation strategy. But do you really understand their wants and needs? Most organizations do not. Go beyond focus groups, surveys, and data mining. Understand their unarticulated and subconscious pains. Once you do this, you can build an innovation strategy that allows you to differentiate your organization and dominate the competition.

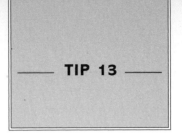

Lessons from Indiana Jones

In 1989's *Indiana Jones and the Last Crusade*, the nerdy archaeology professor Indiana Jones advises students to "forget any ideas you've got about lost cities, exotic travel and digging up the world. We do not follow maps to buried treasure, and 'X' never, ever marks the spot."

Although Dr. Jones is an academic, he is really more of an adventurer. He travels the world uncovering lost civilizations and finding buried treasures.

In today's world of data mining and customer analytics, it can be easy to study your customers from the comfort of your desk. And this somewhat "academic" approach will certainly give you insights into your customers' buying habits, usability behaviors, and other consumer patterns. But most likely you are only gathering data about *your* customers. As a result, you are missing the data of former customers and people who never were customers. As for your current customers, you will only be able to analyze their activities associated with your existing products and services; you won't be able to identify unarticulated needs.

The real treasure can be found when you leave your office, don your fedora and bullwhip, and study customers with your own two eyes.

Anthropologists and innovation experts call this ethnography, a term used to describe any research where the purpose is to provide an in-depth description of everyday life and practices.

Instead of asking your customers questions or analyzing data, you observe them. By doing this you can find out their unarticulated wants and needs. Make sure you listen to lost customers and potential customers as well as current customers. Information from defecting customers can flag changes in customer tastes and the competitive environment or a slippage in some aspect of your organization's value proposition (e.g., quality problems), while potential customers can suggest new sources of value.

One client of mine decided to try this approach. It publishes textbooks for students and instruction manuals for teachers and professors. It wasn't until the publisher started to watch the teachers in the classroom that it developed some interesting product enhancements. For example, during one ethnographic study, it found that teachers lugged several extremely heavy books from class to class. This led the publisher to create a segmented version of the instruction manuals. This enabled teachers to carry only the section of the book they needed that week instead of an entire semester's worth of paper. It is worth noting that teachers never made this suggestion during surveys and focus groups.

These studies can also lead to interesting process improvements. A manufacturer of copying machines wanted to speed up the time it took for a technician to perform copier repairs. While observing customers using their equipment, the company discovered that most repairs were relatively simple, but customers were clueless as to how to fix the problem on their own. The solution? They supplied customers with detailed instructions on how to fix the most common jamming problems so that the customers, not technicians, could solve those problems immediately.

Whirlpool developed pedestals and storage units for its Duet front-loading washers and dryers by observing a woman who had placed her dryer upon cinder blocks to make it easier to load and unload without having to bend over. Although the primary benefit of pedestals is to raise the appliances about a foot off the floor, making it easier to load and unload, the additional weight also helps anchor the machine, minimizing "washer walk." In addition, the drawers that slide out from the pedestals provide an out-of-the-way space to store bottles of laundry detergent, bleach, and fabric softener.

Get out from behind your computer and see the world—and your customers—with fresh eyes. In doing this you are sure to discover opportunities you never expected. And in the process you might just find gold.

The real treasure is found when you leave your office, don your fedora and bullwhip, and study customers with your own two eyes.

Your Market Research Sucks

Imagine you are a hearing aid manufacturer and you want to develop the next generation of product. You conduct surveys and focus groups and discover that nearly 80 percent of the hearing-impaired population, despite the recommendations of their health-care providers, refuse to wear hearing aids, mainly citing cost as the key reason. What do you do?

The obvious answer is to find ways of producing a lower-cost hearing aid. Or is it?

Oticon, a large global manufacturer of hearing aids, wasn't convinced. It realized that its market research only gathered information at a "conscious" level: what the consumers said to it in focus groups and surveys. But the company wanted deeper insights. So it employed a number of techniques for tapping into the subconscious minds of potential customers.

It eventually discovered the real reason people did not want to wear a hearing aid: It made consumers feel flawed, stigma-tized, and old, especially those individuals with early stages of hearing loss in their forties and fifties.

Although making the devices even smaller or nearly invisible might seem like the right answer, further research found that this would only reinforce the consumers' negative feelings, as it confirmed in their minds that a hearing aid was something to be ashamed of.

Based on these new insights, Oticon took a very different route: It made large yet fashionable hearing aids that looked more like earrings and were offered in bright colors and patterns, from the colors of one's alma mater to zebra stripes. During a trial study of people who wore the device for a few weeks, some users said their friends mistook their hearing aids for Bluetooth headsets. In the end, the product was a hit with consumers and even won several design awards.

What Oticon learned was that what consumers say in surveys and focus groups often contradicts what they actually think and feel and how they will ultimately act. The key is to tap into the subconscious minds of your customers, because it is the subconscious mind that really drives behavior.

YOUR CUSTOMERS DON'T KNOW
WHAT THEY DON'T KNOW

Innovators looking for input from consumers must assume that consumers cannot always (and may not want to) explain themselves, their behaviors, their attitudes, and their decision-making processes. The average person is only aware of about 5 percent of his or her thoughts and feelings on any given topic. When asked outright, consumers will, of course, provide answers, but those answers may be incomplete at best and quite misleading at worst. How often have you heard representative consumers say in response to a direct question, "I will definitely buy this product," only to see the product fail (think New Coke, the 1985 reformulation of Coca-Cola that was a huge failure in spite of positive focus group feedback)? Innovators need to find ways to bypass the rational, explicit, conscious mind and tap into the subconscious.

One way to do this is through the use of metaphors and storytelling. Humans think and speak in metaphors. According to Kendall Haven, author of *Story Proof*, in the English language, five to six metaphors are used per minute in everyday speech. Just try expressing yourself, your ideas, your emotions and attitudes without the use of metaphors. It is almost impossible and certainly makes for a very bland conversation. Note that even the word "bland" is a metaphor in this context. Metaphors are based on human experiences and help us make sense of the world.

When Oticon wanted to overcome the shortcoming of focus groups and other traditional market-research techniques, it decided to use a metaphor-driven approach called the Zaltman Metaphor Elicitation Technique (ZMET). This involves in-depth one-on-one interviews and helps consumers express their vision of how a product might fit into their lives, fill a need, or solve a problem. Lindsay Zaltman, managing director of Olson Zaltman, the consulting firm that conducted Oticon's research, found that wearing a hearing aid was like having "a neon sign on your forehead saying, 'I'm flawed, I'm old.'" Now, that's a pretty powerful metaphor.

Designworks USA, a division of BMW, uses a different approach to capture the subconscious needs of consumers. While designing cars and other products such as cell phones, computers, and tractors, instead of starting with the basic functions and features, the company has consumers tell it stories about emotion. Its designers first meet with company executives, employees, and customers in order to capture the emotion that customers will *feel* when they use this product. This is done using sketch artists rather than words. Only after everyone agrees on these emotions will the design of the form and style begin.

According to an Accenture study of executives in 639 companies, the number one reason for innovation failure was that products and services "failed to meet customer needs." Innovators tend to build solutions around the explicitly articulated needs of consumers, often based on numerical data. But in doing so, the "real" consumer needs are missed. As innovators, we need to tap into the darkest recesses of the mind in order to capture what the consumer really wants.

> The average person is only aware of about 5 percent of his or her thoughts and feelings on any given topic. When asked outright, consumers will, of course, provide answers, but those answers may be incomplete at best and quite misleading at worst.

Be the Aspirin for
Your Customers' Pains

We are a country preoccupied with weight loss. What can innovators gain from studying this national obsession?

When scanning men's health magazines, there are two headlines we see over and over: "Lose Your Gut Fast" and "Get Six-Pack Abs." But which of these headlines is more likely to sell magazines?

Although most people intuitively think that the second headline, "Get Six-Pack Abs," is the sure winner, when a Web site did a comparison, it found that "Lose Your Gut Fast" was read significantly more times.

Why?

MEET PEOPLE WHERE THEY ARE

This phenomenon is explained nicely by the Austrian economist Ludwig von Mises, who once said that three requirements must be present for an individual to change:

- The individual must be dissatisfied with the current state of affairs.
- The individual must see a better state.
- The individual must believe that he or she can reach that better state.

That last point is critical as it relates to the "gut" issue. When someone is twenty pounds overweight, six-pack abs are desirable but seem inconceivable. Only when your gut is gone will six-pack abs seem like a possibility. In fact, a follow-up study found that the people most interested in getting six-pack abs were those who did not have a gut.

This is an important concept as it relates to innovation. You must "meet people where they are." That is, you need to solve a pain that they have (e.g., a gut) before you can get them excited about any other gain (e.g., six-pack abs).

LOSSES VERSUS GAINS

This concept is further illustrated by a question I ask my audiences whenever I give a speech. Which would you prefer?

Option 1: a guaranteed gain of $75,000?

Option 2: an 80 percent chance of gaining $100,000, with a 20 percent chance of getting nothing?

When I ask the audience this question, 75 percent choose option 1. This percentage is consistent across all groups, regardless of who is in the audience.

What about the following? Which would you choose?

Option 3: a certain loss of $75,000?

Option 4: an 80 percent chance of losing $100,000, with a 20 percent chance of not losing anything?

When audiences answer this one, 99 percent choose option 4.

Option 1 is about playing it safe when a gain is at stake. Option 4 is about taking risks when a loss is at stake.

Interestingly, when you look at these options, even though most people choose options 1 and 4, options 2 and 3 probabilistically give you better returns. On average, you will gain $80,000 with option 2 and will lose $80,000 with option 4.

In general, people will take greater risks to minimize (or reduce) their pain/losses yet are risk averse when the option is to increase their pleasure/gain.

Advertising agencies know this well. For example, instead of providing peace of mind, insurance companies paint a picture of what would be lost if a catastrophic event occurred and the person was not insured.

Activists are also aware of this. According to author Barry Schwartz, "Appeals to women to do breast self-exams that emphasize the benefits of early cancer detection (gains) are less effective than those that emphasize the costs of late detection (losses)."

Instead of selling customers on how great your product or service is, show them the downside of using a less reliable alternative. When selling her high-priced service, one colleague asks, "If you needed open-heart surgery, would you shop for a cardiologist based on price?" She then launches into the risk associated with not using her top-notch service.

Why is this knowledge important for innovation?

ELIMINATE A PAIN AND THEY WILL COME

We often hear the expression "Build it and they will come." With innovation, a more accurate statement is "Eliminate a pain and they will come." The ultimate success of the automated teller machine (ATM) is a great example of this.

In the mid-1970s, Citibank was the second-largest bank. In 1977, after investing hundreds of millions of dollars in ATM technology research and development, Citibank decided to install machines across all of New York City. At first they were not very popular. The technology was confusing to first-time users, the machines were not always accurate (they sometimes dispensed the wrong amount of money), and they were impersonal. According to one person involved in the ATM rollout, customers who used ATMs were so frustrated that many closed their Citibank accounts.

The ATM might never have been a hit if it hadn't been for a natural disaster.

February 1978 will always be remembered for a blizzard that dumped as much as four feet of snow in the Northeast. In New York City, nearly two feet of snow brought the city to a grinding halt. Banks weren't open. Instead, people got their money by cashing checks at local supermarkets. But most of the supermarkets quickly ran out of money.

This created a massive "pain."

Where did people turn? The ATMs. It is estimated that during the storms, use of the machines increased by over 20 percent. Soon after, Citibank started running TV ads showing people trudging through the snowdrifts in New York City. That's when the company introduced its wildly popular slogan, "The Citi Never Sleeps." This was the real birth of the automated teller machine.

By 1981, Citibank's market share of New York deposits had doubled, with a lot of the growth attributed to the ATM.

This story illustrates an innovator's dilemma and opportunity. Brilliant innovations are not necessarily adopted by the masses, and some ideas just need time to incubate and gain acceptance. But will your business survive long enough to see the success?

People take massive risks to eliminate their pains but play it safe when it comes to adding convenience. ATMs were primarily about convenience. What did it take for them to become a success? A pain caused by a natural disaster.

Think about the last mattress commercial you heard. They all say the same thing: "Buy our XYZ bed and you will get your best night's sleep ever." Yawn. Boring. The commercial may put me to sleep, but it's not going to get me to buy a bed.

Now consider this actual radio advertisement. "If your mattress is ten years old, it weighs twice its original weight due to the dust mites that accumulate over the years." Ouch! This creates a pain and makes me want to replace my mattress immediately.

Are your new ideas solving a problem? If they are just a convenience, what can you do to take advantage of a pain—without having to rely on a natural disaster?

We often hear the expression "Build it and they will come." But with innovation, a more accurate statement is "Eliminate a pain and they will come."

Innovate Where You Differentiate

In his book *Animal Farm*, George Orwell writes, "All animals are equal, but some animals are more equal than others."

This is an important mantra to remember when creating an innovation program. All capabilities are equal, but some are more equal than others. You don't innovate the same way for each capability in your business. And the way you innovate will not be the same as the way your competitors innovate.

When I conduct executive training, one of my favorite activities requires participants to consider a typical set of capabilities common in the insurance industry: developing products and services, customer service, managing revenues, managing distribution channels, marketing products and services, underwriting, claims fulfillment, managing provider networks, and planning and managing the enterprise.

I then ask the group to tell me which capability is the most important to an insurance company. Quite often, the first answer will be claims fulfillment. "Why?" I ask, and they say, "Because this is why customers get insurance in the first place." I agree that claims fulfillment is very important, but it is not the *most* important.

Someone will then suggest managing revenues (or underwriting) because this is how the company makes money. Again, I commend them for their answer, but it is still not the most important capability. After nearly every process has been suggested, I stop the group and say, "Okay, I am going to give you the answer to this one: 'It depends.'"

DIFFERENT STROKES FOR DIFFERENT FOLKS

Consider four insurance companies serving relatively similar markets.

- *Unum Insurance:* Unum is the market leader in disability insurance, a firm that differentiates itself by assessing and pricing risk. Unum claims, for example, to have such finely tuned data that it can distinguish the difference in risk between left-handed and right-handed doctors who drive Volvos and live in New Jersey.
- *Progressive Insurance:* In the late 1990s, when Progressive decided to compete against the bigger players, it chose to do so by changing the way claims were processed, becoming one of the most profitable firms in the industry. Progressive's loss adjusters operate from vans with cellular communication links and computer workstations. Driving around their assigned territories, they are often at the scene of an accident before the police. In many cases, claims are processed on the spot, and the company's loss adjusters have been known to hand over a check at the site of an accident.
- *State Farm:* Competitive positioning for State Farm depends on its exclusive (and extensive) network of agents and offices.

Its wide geographic coverage is reinforced by its motto: "Like a Good Neighbor, State Farm Is There." The firm differentiates itself from the rest of the pack through this slogan and network.

• *USAA:* The customers of USAA are primarily in the transient, mobile military services, and the company is known for providing great help to this niche group. At one time, USAA was the world's largest user of toll-free numbers, which it used as the main means to communicate with customers. All of its innovation efforts focus on making the lives of its customers (called "members") better. These investments have paid off, as *BusinessWeek* continually ranks USAA one of the top companies in customer service.

What is the most important capability to Unum? It is underwriting. For Progressive, its source of differentiation is claims fulfillment. For State Farm, its distribution network is critical because it deals with a broad swath of the population. Lastly, USAA is focused on customer service. Capabilities that are strategic for one organization may well be less critical for another in the same industry. All four of these companies are essentially in the same business, but each concentrates on a different capability to achieve a competitive advantage in the marketplace.

What is *your* most important capability? When I ask this question of CEOs, other top executives, and employees, there is typically a very long, uncomfortable silence. Most people do not think of their business in these terms. But as you will see in the next tip, clearly defining your focus will help you allocate your innovation investments.

Of course, this does not mean that you only need to excel at one part of your business. The purpose is to help you identify your differentiators, which will often change over time. For example, Progressive Insurance is currently best known not for its Immediate Response Vehicles but rather for its ability to offer quotes of its competitors along with its own.

So what is your most important capability? Although the question is simple, the answer requires significant reflection and alignment, and answering it is important for determining your innovation strategy. In particular, it helps you focus your limited innovation investments on the capabilities that will yield the greatest impact.

All capabilities are equal, but some are more equal than others. You don't innovate the same way for each capability in your business. And the way you innovate will not be the same as the way your competitors innovate.

—— TIP 17 ——

Ever Notice How "One Size Fits All" Never Really Fits All?

Once you identify your "most important" capability, you can use this information to develop your operating strategy—the way in which you run your business. Below is a simple framework called the Innovation Targeting Matrix (ITM) that I use to help organizations identify the right strategies for their business.

DIFFERENTIATING	Innovate
CORE	Automate Simplify Outsource
SUPPORT	Eliminate Minimize Outsource

The ITM illustrates how capabilities fall into three levels of strategic importance (from least to most strategic): "support," "core," and "differentiating."

Support capabilities are necessary for running the business yet are not your core business. Quite often these are things like HR, IT, or finance.

- *Operating Strategy:* Support work should be minimized and, ideally, outsourced as much as possible.
- Cost containment is the main strategy while still ensuring high quality.

Core capabilities are critical to your business but are not your source of competitive advantage. These create direct value for the customer. For a manufacturing company, core capabilities might include order fulfillment, order acquisition, and product support. Quite often these capabilities are "transactional" in nature.

- *Operating Strategy:* Core work should be simplified and automated whenever possible. The objective is to turn these capabilities into well-oiled machines.
- Efficiency is the main strategy.

Differentiating capabilities are those that set you apart from your competition. These are your most important capabilities, as described in the previous tip. Ideally, you have only one or two of these capabilities. At USAA, for example, this is customer service.

- *Operating Strategy:* Differentiating work is typically knowledge work and is where you want to make the greatest investment. Ideally, you want to empower knowledge workers to deliver non-cookie-cutter results that will continually set you apart from your competitors.
- Innovation is the main strategy.

There are several important points to note with this model:

• **Make Sure Your Core Is Working Before You Innovate:** Because innovation seems glamorous, companies often try to focus on differentiators before they have a good foundation. This is a mistake. You must have your "core" capabilities working well (efficient, low error rates, high service levels) before you can start worrying about your differentiators.

• **Use This Targeting Approach at Every Level:** This model is valuable not just at the enterprise level but also within each capability. Even support capabilities have components that help differentiate the company. For example, a major consulting firm was reevaluating its corporate training curriculum and used this model to assist in the process. It first determined which classes provided capabilities necessary to beat the competition— that is, its training "differentiators." For these, in-house custom courses were developed with the help of leading universities and thought leaders. For "core" consultant skills, the firm partnered with world-class training organizations to provide tailored versions of existing training. And for less important, support skills, it used off-the-shelf training modules (outsourced training).

• *Recognize That Technology Can Be a Differentiator:* Sometimes your differentiating capability can be one that ensures that the work of others is repeatable and predictable. These can be capabilities that we might ordinarily think of as support: IT, finance, or HR. For example, Wal-Mart invests heavily in the ability to connect stores, warehouses, and vendors through leading-edge technology. The employees who develop these computer systems are some of Wal-Mart's most valuable knowledge workers.

• *You Can't Catch Your Competition:* If you are number two or number three (or worse) in your industry, your differentiating capability should ideally be different from that of your leading competitors. When you are playing catch-up, changing the rules of the game is critical. It is hard to beat someone at *their* game.

• *Your Differentiators Should Be Difficult to Replicate:* If your differentiating capability is easy for your competition to replicate, it probably is not a differentiator. One company that offers service warranties on water heaters and other appliances claimed its "offerings"—the bundling and pricing of its services—were its competitive differentiator. When I asked the group, "How long after introducing a new offering does your competition offer the same deal?" I discovered that the answer was "In as little as two weeks." Clearly that was not a good differentiator. After digging further, we found that the company's deep relationships with its third-party repair technicians were distinctive and unassailable. This was a great differentiator. Unless you want to reinvent yourself on a weekly basis, you should find a differentiator that is difficult to replicate and is uniquely yours.

Understanding your differentiators is important. This is a key component of any company's business strategy. And it is equally important to know how those differentiators translate into your innovation strategy. This helps cascade priorities down to the lowest levels of the organization. It helps to focus investments on the areas of innovation that will create the greatest returns. And it helps you determine which challenges will most likely move the needle forward for your organization.

> It is important to know how your differentiators translate into your innovation strategy. This helps cascade priorities down to the lowest levels of the organization.

TIP 18

Best Practices Are (Sometimes) Stupid

I play golf—not well, but I play golf. My handicap is in the double digits. For me to shoot par would be a dream. But for Tiger Woods, par would be a nightmare. I am reminded of this comparison when I see companies that are satisfied to focus on their understanding of "par," otherwise known as best practice. It was once an admirable aim, but it is not sufficient today. Your competitors are more like Tiger Woods than they are like me. Par won't keep you alive in the current environment. Once something becomes a best practice, it is really no longer a best practice.

Innovation is about adaptability, your ability to change in order to stay one step ahead of the competition. When you copy someone's best practice, you are not staying ahead; you are playing a game of catch-up. Your differentiating capability, in particular, must be unique and distinctive and not based on what others are doing. When Progressive Insurance wanted to compete with the "big boys," it did not use best practices; it created the Immediate Response Vehicles, something unique to the industry.

THE BEST USE FOR BEST PRACTICES

However, having said that, I am not against best practices altogether. I am just against using them as your innovation strategy for your "differentiating" capabilities.

Here are a few places where best practice can be useful:

• *Core and Support:* Best practices can actually be useful for core and support capabilities (see the previous tip). These capabilities should run like a well-oiled machine with high quality and low cost. But these capabilities will not help you stand out in a crowded marketplace.

• *Best Practices from Outside Your Industry:* You can get some incredible innovations from companies that are not your competition. In fact, I encourage you to "steal with pride" from companies outside your industry. For example, Southwest Airlines did this when it benchmarked an Indianapolis 500 pit crew to improve plane turnaround time. Hospitals have gained new insights by studying the check-in process of hotels. And a mail-order office supply company improved the return of empty toner cartridges by applying Netflix's DVD subscription process. Sometimes these cross-industry best practices can be revolutionary.

• *Innovation:* Although you want to focus your innovation efforts on *your* differentiating capabilities, unless you are an innovation company (like IDEO or InnoCentive), *how* you innovate is probably not a differentiator. For example, if you are an insurance company, you want to apply innovation to your claims processing if claims processing is a differentiator. But the innovation process is only a core capability. There is no point in your inventing new innovation methods. Therefore, you should use innovation best practices wherever and whenever possible. Reading this book will give you a number of those best practices.

Best practices are not an innovation strategy. Copying the competition will only help you achieve parity. Only when you fully understand your innovation targeting strategy can you determine where best practices are useful and where they are truly a waste of time.

> Your competitors are like Tiger Woods. Par (aka best practice) won't keep you alive in the current environment.

Simplification Is the Best Innovation

Antoine de Saint-Exupéry, author of *The Little Prince*, once said, "Perfection is finally attained not when there is no longer anything to add but when there is no longer anything to take away."

Unfortunately, most innovators believe that perfection involves adding as many features and functions as possible. As a result, all too often new products are overly complex and end up "overserving" their customers.

Microsoft Office is a perfect example of this. While 99 percent of the software's functionality goes unused, these complexities slow down the computer and reduce ease of use. Being able to do everything for everyone is not perfection.

MAKE YOUR PRODUCTS MORE ACCESSIBLE

Instead, focus on making your products more accessible. "Accessible" can have a variety of meanings.

The video game market has always been enamored with increasingly faster machines and higher-quality graphics. But the Nintendo Wii changed that. Instead of creating more sophisticated and complicated games that would appeal to the advanced gamer, Nintendo created an interface that would appeal to people ages eight and eighty alike. That's accessibility. In 2008, 10.2 million Wii units were sold in the United States, compared to only 4.7 million Xbox 360s and 3.5 million PlayStation 3s. And there was a significant amount of money being made on all of the Wii add-ons. Since then, competitors like Xbox 360's Kinect have been quick to replicate the Wii's success, creating a whole new level of competition.

Service-based organizations can make their offerings more affordable and accessible by turning them into physical or digital products that require little or no human intervention.

- Cybersettle automates insurance claims processing.
- My Personality Poker cards enable people to re-create one of my most popular presentations at a fraction of the cost.
- Self-assessment tools can reduce reliance on consultants.
- Remote diagnostic technologies can speed medical exams and prequalify patients before they come to the doctor.
- PlumChoice.com enables technicians to fix computers through remote access, saving customers money and eliminating the need to bring the machine to the repair store.
- LegalZoom.com offers affordable legal advice for people who might otherwise not seek counsel.
- TurboTax simplifies tax filing.
- Ernst & Young Consulting (now Capgemini) once offered a subscription service, Ernie, that provided small businesses with a low-cost online alternative to high-priced consulting.

- Experts convert their intellectual property into books, MP3s, DVDs, digitally delivered training (including e-learning) systems, or online databases.

And the possibilities are endless.

Another option is to develop a low-cost version of your products and services. Examine why people are really using your products/services and the bare minimum ways of delivering the desired outcome. Three-hundred-dollar netbooks are popular because they are stripped-down computers and most people just want to do word processing and surf the Net. Apple's iPad takes this one step further by making an intuitive user interface in an incredibly light product, making it accessible to both technophiles and technophobes alike. And for the first time, smartphones are now outselling computers.

Dow Corning, the maker of silicone-based products, has traditionally been in the low-volume, high-service business. To make its product more accessible and affordable, it launched a high-volume, low-service business. This business sells purely through the Internet, with no call centers, and the product can only be ordered in bulk. Although this model cannibalized some of Dow Corning's core business, on the whole it grew the entire business considerably, giving the company access to buyers who would never have used it previously.

Which features, services, or qualities can be reduced in order to tap into a new market?

Michelangelo once said, "In every block of marble I see a statue as plain as though it stood before me, shaped and perfect in attitude and action. I have only to hew away the rough walls that imprison the lovely apparition to reveal it to the other eyes as mine see it." My guess is your masterpiece is being covered up by a lot of useless features, functions, and expensive services.

"Perfection is finally attained not when there is no longer anything to add but when there is no longer anything to take away."—Antoine de Saint-Exupéry

Innovation Measures and Motivation

All executives know that measurements are important to running any business. But do your measures stimulate ingenuity and foster efficient innovation? Or are they inadvertently killing creativity and encouraging less-than-desirable behaviors? Successful innovation requires an understanding of psychology, neuroscience, motivational theory, and the scientific method. Armed with this information you can motivate people to participate in innovation and minimize the risks associated with failure.

Motivate Like Maslow

Skeeball is an arcade game where players "bowl" for points. During my childhood, it was hugely popular. Why? What motivated kids to part with their hard-earned allowance money to play this game? Of course it was fun. But more important, it was one of the first arcade games to give you tickets based on the number of points you got. These could be redeemed for silly prizes like candy, fake vampire fangs, or rubber spiders. Although the most desirable prizes required thousands of tickets and were out of the reach of nearly every player, we played anyway, cherishing each ticket that we won.

The motivation technique that got us as children to part with our quarters is still being used in corporations today to get people to participate in innovation efforts. Let's explore a few of the most popular methods.

EXTRINSIC MOTIVATORS

Although cash bonuses for innovations have been around for ages, more sophisticated methods have gained popularity recently. One involves the use of a points system. When you contribute an idea or solution, comment, or vote, you get points—much like American Express Membership Rewards points or skeeball tickets—that can be used to buy a variety of items: company T-shirts, mugs, and other "exciting" items.

Some companies have taken the concept a bit further and allow people to accumulate points that can be used in auctions. Once a month the company holds an auction for a trip to, say, Tahiti. Anyone with points can join the bidding. This encourages people to earn and save as many points as possible so that they can have a chance at some really big prizes.

Another model that doesn't necessarily need a points system involves "priceless" awards. Remember the MasterCard commercials? Dinner with the CEO, a prime parking space, or an extra week of vacation; these types of prizes are great motivators because no amount of money can buy them.

All of these models have an extrinsic form of motivation in common. They all offer a tangible prize. Chip Conley, author of *Peak*, would point out that these motivators relate to the lowest rungs on Abraham Maslow's hierarchy of needs—five levels of human needs where higher-level needs are not felt until lower-level needs have been satisfied. The lowest two levels involve physiology (e.g., food and shelter) and safety/security. Extrinsic motivations, such as money, allow you to meet these basic human needs. (See graphic at the top of the next page.)

Yet there is an opportunity for other, potentially more effective forms of motivation for innovation.

THE WORK IS ITS OWN REWARD

At the highest level of Maslow's hierarchy, you find "self-actualization." In the innovation/business world, this is where

"the work is its own reward." The open-source software movement has largely been built on this model. Millions of people help develop software without any formal extrinsic compensation. Many do it just because it "feels good to contribute." For some, it is about building software that will bring down the "evil empire" (aka Microsoft).

While working in Formula 1—ultrafast car racing—I learned the power of this highest level of motivation. At the manufacturing plant where the cars are produced, the job is similar to that of workers at traditional automotive manufacturers. But the race team employees work longer hours, often for less pay than their traditional counterparts. Why? They love their job. It's not *what* they are doing that matters. It is *why* they are doing it that motivates them. Being part of a winning racing team spurs them to perform at their best. Although this "work is its own reward" is an incredibly effective motivator in some situations, it is difficult to put into practice inside a typical organization.

STATUS AND RECOGNITION

There is a third type of motivation that lies between safety/physiology and self-actualization and relates to Maslow's love/belonging and self-esteem: status and recognition. This can be extremely effective, especially inside organizations where people are hired mainly for their degrees and intelligence.

For some individuals, being recognized, by their peers in particular, is the highest form of motivation. In some circles, being published in a peer-reviewed journal is one of the highest honors to be bestowed on someone.

Therefore, find ways of recognizing people, especially when it involves peer recognition. The name of the game is status.

One way to do this, if you use a points system like the ones described above, is to create a leader board. This creates friendly competition in the workplace and helps individuals stand out from the crowd based on their contributions.

Another approach, of course, is to develop a good recognition program as part of your communication plans. Many companies do this, but they rarely do it well.

Here's the real opportunity. . . .

STOP RECOGNIZING PEOPLE FOR DOING THEIR JOBS

Stop recognizing people for doing their jobs. When you hire someone to work for you, it should be expected that they have a basic level of competence. When you recognize people for doing what they are hired to do, it reinforces a culture where the status quo is good enough.

Instead, recognize and reward people for going beyond their jobs and for doing things that are unexpected.

If you want to encourage open innovation or cross-business-unit collaboration, then recognize people for that. If you want employees to take risks, make a big deal out of individuals who do so. If you want to let people know that failure is acceptable—when done the right way—then highlight situations where something didn't work as planned yet powerful lessons were learned.

When you shift the conversations throughout your organization, you begin to change the culture. These types of motivation programs are a great opportunity to create an environment of innovation and promote the values that are important to your organization.

There is no one-size-fits-all approach to motivating employees. Each individual has different needs and wants. But when done properly, a good recognition-and-rewards program can make the skeeball model of motivation seem like child's play.

Stop recognizing people for doing their jobs. When you hire someone to work for you, it should be expected that they are competent. When you recognize people for doing what they are hired to do, it reinforces a culture where the status quo is good enough.

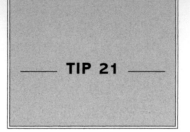

TIP 21

You Get What You Measure, but Will You Get What You Want?

In business, there is an old adage, "You get what you measure." But the big question is, will you get what you want? Too many innovation-measurement systems are designed in a way that inadvertently creates undesirable behaviors. They measure the wrong things, resulting in poor results.

In general, there are four types of innovation measures:

1. *Activity/Capability Measures*—These measure the activity associated with participation in your challenges and the overall innovation program (e.g., number of registered solvers, number of submissions per challenge, percentage of time invested in innovation, percentage of employees trained in innovation).

2. *Solve-Rate Measures*—These subjectively measure how well you solved your challenges (e.g., percentage of challenges partially solved, percentage of challenges completely solved, potential value of solutions).

3. *Implementation Measures*—Finding solutions to your challenges is not enough. You need to implement the solutions in

a cost-effective and timely manner (e.g., percentage of solutions implemented, time to market, implementation costs, percentage of on-time product launches).

4. *Value Realization Measures*—These measure the actual value accrued (e.g., increase in revenues, reduction in costs, percentage of revenue from innovations introduced in last six months, overall ROI).

Of course we want our innovation efforts to result in value—the last measure—as this is where the rubber meets the road. But sometimes value realization can take years, or, in the case of pharmaceutical companies, decades. Therefore, you need the first three measures as a way of monitoring progress with your program in the short term. These are leading indicators that can help predict long-term success.

The first category—activity and capability—is useful in measuring trends over time for things like community engagement, effectiveness of internal communications, and quality of challenges. But sometimes measuring activity can be misleading.

When working with clients, one of the most common activity measures is the number of solutions submitted for a given challenge. But this often leads to misleading results. Which is better: getting one hundred solutions or getting only two solutions? Although most people intuitively think that one hundred is better than two, this is not necessarily true. As pointed out earlier, it is not the absolute number that matters but rather the proportion of good solutions to bad solutions. If you received one hundred solutions where only two of them were exactly what you needed and the other ninety-eight were duds, this would be worse than getting just two that were right on the money.

Although a lot of activity is good, too many submissions can indicate that you have a poorly defined challenge. Remember that a well-defined challenge is one that is self-vetting, preventing too many poor submissions from even making it into the system. The solar activity challenge run by NASA yielded only four solutions, but one of those solutions was spot-on. Therefore, the ratio of good solutions to duds (aka the signal-to-noise ratio) might be a more interesting measure.

The key is to make sure you understand the unintended consequences of your measurement system, especially when it comes to activity measures. If used properly, these measures can help you drive higher solve rates (measure number two).

DIAGNOSING PERFORMANCE

But higher solve rates do not always lead to greater value (measure number four). High solve rates with low value can indicate problems with your innovation program:

- *Poor implementation*—You are unable to convert solutions into finished products/services.
- *Poor commercialization*—Your solutions do not meet the needs of the market/customers and therefore do not generate revenue.
- *Poor relevance*—Your challenges, although solved, are not important enough to "move the needle" of the organization's innovation efforts.

Measures are important for helping track your innovation efforts, and they can help diagnose potential issues, but it is important to measure the right things. Simply shifting what you measure can significantly impact the results.

Consider the typical product-development process. Research and development (R&D) people are the only ones held accountable, often developing solutions from their ivory towers. Their solutions may or may not meet customer needs and often do not meet internal business needs. One of Europe's leading medical manufacturers, in an effort to fix this problem, shifted to cross-functional teams with joint responsibility for the end result. Now product development no longer finishes at product definition. It continues until three months after product launch. Sales, marketing, manufacturing, legal, vendor management, and others are involved in this cross-functional effort. As a result, nearly 70 percent of the company's new products launch on time, compared with just 15 percent previously.

Peter Drucker once said, "If you can't measure it, you can't manage it." Yes, measures play an important role in innovation. They give a snapshot of performance, they provide early detection of potential issues, and they drive behaviors. The key is to use the right measures in a way that helps, rather than hinders, innovation.

Too many innovation-measurement systems are designed in a way that inadvertently creates undesirable behaviors.

The Performance Paradox

If you want to go faster, stop focusing on speed. If you want to be more creative, stop measuring creativity. Paradoxically, when organizations hyperfocus on their goals, they are less likely to achieve those goals.

Let's think back to the Formula 1 racing team example for a moment. Although the cars are technological marvels, it was the pit crews that always amazed me most. Back when I worked with them, a pit crew consisted of twenty men who serviced the race cars, refueling, changing tires, and performing required maintenance in a matter of seconds. To ensure that each pit crew member was in the right role, team members would continually shift positions during practice until they found the optimal configuration of the team. A stopwatch measured their time in milliseconds. As they practiced, there came a point where no matter how hard they tried, they couldn't go any faster. Not even one one-thousandth of a second faster. This was their performance plateau, their best possible time.

Then, as an experiment, the pit crew boss told the team to concentrate *not* on their time but rather on their style. They were asked to think the word "smooth" while changing the tires. This time, their movements were more significant than their speed.

Astonishingly, when they weren't focusing on speed, the crew shaved several tenths of a second off their best time, even though they "felt" that they were going slower.

I call this the performance paradox. It occurs when overly focusing on a future goal (e.g., beating the stopwatch) may be the very thing that prevents you (and your team) from hitting your targets.

Although the general concept of counterintuitive motivation has gained pop culture status recently, due to books like *Drive* by Dan Pink, the research in this area goes back to the turn of the century.

In the early 1900s, Robert Yerkes and J. D. Dodson developed the aptly named Yerkes-Dodson law. The premise is that performance increases relative to motivation (they called it "arousal") only to a point, after which performance drops. Then, as you become "overmotivated," performance paradoxically decreases. Typically, this progression is drawn as an inverted U-shaped curve.

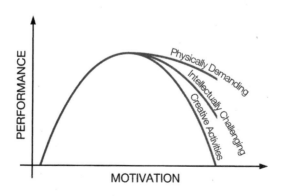

The key is to find the sweet spot of optimal performance. And this usually involves a focus on the activity, not the target or goal.

Yerkes and Dodson suggested that different tasks require different levels of arousal (to use their word). For example, physically demanding tasks often require higher levels of motivation. This explains why professional athletes are inclined to be more goal driven. Even so, as demonstrated by the pit crew example, too much goal orientation will hurt even athletic performance.

Within the business world, Yerkes and Dodson found that to improve concentration, intellectually challenging tasks required lower levels of arousal/motivation. And the more creative the activity, the less motivation was required to hit peak levels of performance.

In fact, studies reveal that creativity often diminishes when individuals are rewarded (externally/extrinsically motivated) for doing their work. Why? The desire to achieve the goal overtakes the personal interest in the endeavor.

If a reward—money, awards, or even praise—becomes the reason for engaging in an activity, the endeavor will ultimately be viewed as less enjoyable in its own right and the focus will shift to getting the task done quickly with minimal risk. This overshadows the intellectual stimulation of the process and kills creativity. Creativity is a process that cannot be forced.

Dr. Teresa Amabile of Harvard University once wrote that "rewards undermine creativity when [individuals feel that their] self-determination is undermined." However, "rewards can enhance creativity when they confirm competence, provide useful information in a supportive way, or enable people to do something that they were already intrinsically motivated to do."

This is often best accomplished through measures that make people feel as though they are in control rather than being controlled. Freedom to be creative (rather than mandates to be creative) enhance performance.

What can an organization to do to address this performance paradox?

Just as the pit crew needed to stop focusing on the stopwatch in order to go faster, you and your team need to stop focusing on your goals in order to enhance creativity and performance. This involves "being present"—a concept that is often difficult to embrace.

A high school student I once met had become increasingly anxious over passing her upcoming final exam in math, which was always her weakest subject. She studied incredibly hard, but despite her efforts, she failed. The stress to perform overstimulated her, making it difficult for her to concentrate. In business, we inadvertently do the same when we set tight deadlines and overly aggressive targets.

Fortunately for this student, her teachers gave her another chance. But this time, instead of concentrating on passing (the result), when she woke up each morning, she would visualize herself as Condoleezza Rice, the former U.S. secretary of state and a very successful, highly educated woman. In her mind, Dr. Rice wouldn't worry about a high school math exam, so neither should she. By imagining she was someone else, she stopped agonizing and gained more confidence. By changing her mind-set and not focusing on the result, she reduced her stress and scored 93 percent, her greatest performance to date.

Why does this performance paradox take place? One reason has to do with the wiring of the brain.

The cerebellum is the place where we store practiced skills for automatic recall. Unfortunately, we become less proficient at those practiced skills when we engage the cerebral cortex—the thinking part of the brain. Overthinking kills automatic recall.

For example, say you are an excellent golfer and have practiced your swing hundreds of times. To access those skills, you need to stop thinking about them. When you are in a tournament (a stressful situation), if you try to access those practiced responses by thinking about them, you choke. These stored responses can be accessed only through relaxation. Practiced behaviors enacted in a calm environment can be used with a good deal of proficiency.

The same is true for creativity.

Most individuals are naturally creative, but we often overthink and lose our ability to do what is an innate ability. In essence, we are "choking" our ability to be creative when we think too much, feel too much stress, or are motivated extrinsically.

To increase creativity, first be aware of the impact that stress is having on creativity in your organization. To reduce stress, encourage employees to focus on the process rather than the outcome. Add subjective measures to your performance-management system and measure people on their qualitative contribution to the business, not just the quantitative numbers.

One company I know has its employees meditate outside before embarking on any creative endeavor. Although this might go beyond what most companies are comfortable doing, this company has found that this reduces stress, enhances creativity, and increases overall performance.

John Cleese, best known for his role on the British comedy *Monty Python*, once said, "High creativity is responding to situations without critical thought. . . . If you want creative workers, give them enough time to play."

> If you want to go faster, stop focusing on speed. If you want to be more creative, stop measuring creativity. Paradoxically, when organizations hyperfocus on their goals, they are less likely to achieve those goals.

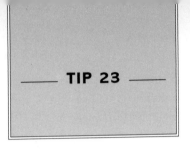

TIP 23

Time Pressure Kills Creativity

A good friend and colleague of mine, Scott Halford, is an authority on neurobehaviorism. He uses a simple yet effective exercise that demonstrates the impact that time pressure can have on creativity.

Although this is a demonstration of how time pressure kills creativity, it is not presented to the audience as such. It is important to pitch it as a test of what the brain is able to hear and process. Here's what you tell the group:

We are going to conduct an experiment that will test how fast your brain works. I will read you a long list of numbers. I want you to write down as many numbers as you can. I will be speaking quite fast, so try to keep up. The person who writes down the most *correct* numbers will be the winner and will get a prize. Interspersed with the numbers will be a command to write something else down. To be eligible for the prize, you must write something, anything, for these. Oh, and based on experiences with other groups, men tend to write down 10 percent more numbers on average than women. One last thing, you don't have the option *not* to compete. Everyone must go for the prize. Ready?

At this point, pull out a sheet of paper. You can write down numbers in advance if you want. But it is just as easy to make up numbers while pretending to read off a blank sheet. Then, in rapid-fire manner, shout out about twenty numbers: 56, 789, 43, 2, 105, 456, 84, etc. Then, without pausing, say, "Write down the first color that comes to mind," and then immediately continue with another list of ten numbers. Then, again without pausing, say, "Write down the first piece of furniture that comes to mind," and continue with another list of ten or so numbers. Then, without pausing, say, "Write down the first genius that comes to mind." Close with a few more numbers and tell people to put down their pens.

Now it is time to see the results. And we won't focus on the numbers but rather on the other commands.

Ask everyone to stand. If they did not write down a color, have them sit down. Most people should be standing. Then say, "If you wrote down blue, red, green, or yellow as the color, please sit down." In most instances, most people will sit. Ask people to list the other colors they wrote down. More than 90 percent of audience members write down these four "primary" colors because these are the colors we've known since we were kids.

Next, ask everyone to stand. If someone did not write down a piece of furniture, have him or her sit down. Then say, "If you wrote down couch, sofa, chair, table, or desk, please sit." Most people will sit at this point. Again, these are the most common pieces of furniture.

Finally, ask everyone to stand one last time. If someone did not write down a genius, have him or her sit down. Then say, "If you wrote down Einstein, please sit down." At this point, nearly everyone will be seated.

Here's the point: When pressed for time, in this case, severely pressed for time, creativity is completely eliminated. Novelty goes out the window. People focus on getting the job done. The fact that this exercise is set up like a competition simulates what is done in many organizations. Extrinsic motivation (the prize and bragging rights) overshadows creativity. Of course, you didn't ask people to be creative. But even if you had, under these circumstances it would have been very difficult.

As a follow-up, ask people to think up a color that no one else will write down. Only give them a few seconds. Now, if you go one by one through the room, you will find a wide divergence of colors, typically two to ten times *more* colors than people write when under pressure (depending on the size of the group). Asking people to be creative and giving them a little breathing room can do wonders to enhance creativity.

This is a great example of how incredible time pressures or extreme stress can kill creativity. In these situations, individuals choose automatic responses that have been programmed into their brains over the years.

Asking people to be creative and giving them a little breathing room can do wonders to enhance creativity.

> Asking people to be creative and giving them a little breathing room can do wonders to enhance creativity.

Failure Is Always an Option

A clothing manufacturer wanted to venture into the direct-to-consumer retail business. Rather than developing a detailed strategy based on years of analysis, it rented an empty space in a local mall and set up a trial shop in a matter of weeks. The store was set up with video cameras and other equipment to help analyze the results. Although the store concept ultimately "failed," the company learned more during two months of running the experiment than it would have spending a year analyzing the marketplace. It quickly reworked the store and tested out a second version, then continued the process with frequent iterations. Over time it increased the size of the experiments until the stores were rolled out on a national level.

Adam Savage, a cohost on the television show *MythBusters*, is known to say, "Failure is *always* an option. It is the cornerstone of our approach to the scientific method. Any result is a result."

This is a profound way to look at innovation.

When you look at and measure life—and innovation—as a series of experiments, failure takes on a whole new meaning.

REDEFINE FAILURE

One definition of an experiment is "a test or investigation, especially one planned to provide evidence for or against a hypothesis."

The only way an experiment can fail is if you don't gather the proper evidence. Even if the evidence proves your hypothesis was wrong, the experiment itself can be considered a huge success, as it will save you a lot of money in the long run. When you view innovation through the lens of experimentation, it redefines failure. Tip 9 ("What Did Edison Get Wrong About Innovation?") might appear to denigrate the value of experimentation. The reality is, *someone* must experiment and "fail." And open innovation is not always appropriate or applicable.

Therefore, when developing new concepts, one approach (especially when "market" uncertainty is involved) is to create small experiments that can be scaled and measured over time. Here are four likely outcomes of an experiment:

1. Our hypothesis was validated by the experiment. Let's make a larger investment in a larger experiment.
2. Our original hypothesis was wrong, but we found a different direction that looks promising. Let's create a new experiment with the new hypothesis.
3. Our original hypothesis was wrong and we should kill the idea.
4. Our experiment did not give us enough data to determine whether or not the hypothesis was correct.

Of these four outcomes, only the last one is a failure. With the other three, the experiment was successful. It becomes a way to measure if we are on the right path, and it stops us from making further investments in the wrong direction.

BUILD IT, TRY IT, FIX IT

One of the biggest barriers to innovation success is analysis paralysis. It is the belief that studying the marketplace ad infinitum will yield better results. This is just not true. We can never predict what will happen in the "real" world, no matter how much data we have, how many focus groups we conduct, or how many strategy consulting firms we hire.

Therefore, instead of using an "analyze, design, build, test, deploy" model, use the "build it, try it, fix it" model—build something, try it out for a while, and learn from your experiments. Each iteration gives you valuable information about the real world, not the spreadsheet world.

It is a simple process and it was the one used by the clothing manufacturer when it wanted to venture into the retail market. Develop a small experiment where the risk associated with failure is limited or controllable (build it). Learn from the results (try it). Adjust the experiment (fix it). Continue to iterate with larger experiments, increasing the scale. Change directions when necessary. Stop pursuing an idea when the experiment suggests a lack of viability or desirability.

Experiments that are done well will focus your energies on opportunities that are market ready, while avoiding unnecessary investments in potential duds.

However, sometimes even well-defined experiments can give you false positives. That is, the experiment tells you a new product, service, or market is a good idea, yet in the end it proves to be a total flop. In those situations, you have a good ol'-fashioned failure on your hands.

Of course, there are productive ways to shine a light on failure. A giant retailer, in its quest for big successes, had some colossal failures. Instead of chastising the people involved with the failed venture, the retailer celebrated. It held a massive funeral. There was even a coffin in which the project (not the project team) was buried.

Several years back, Intuit decided to target a younger population by linking tax filing with hip-hop. It made large marketing investments and created partnerships with companies like Expedia and Best Buy. But in the end, its marketing effort proved unsuccessful and the program was killed. How did the company handle the failure? According to *BusinessWeek*, "The team that developed the campaign documented its insights, such as the fact that Gen Yers don't visit destination Web sites that feel too much like advertising." Then, on a stage, in front of some two hundred Intuit marketers, the team received an award from Intuit chairman Scott Cook, who said, "It's only a failure if we fail to get the learning."

You want to be careful not to glorify failure too much. Successes can give you useful input at a much lower price tag. But if you do fail, deal with the problem head-on and then learn from the experience.

One company that lives and breathes this philosophy is Koch Industries, the second-largest privately held company in the United States, with approximately one hundred billion dollars in annual revenues. Charles Koch, the company's chairman and

CEO, encourages employees to build small experiments that prove or disprove hypotheses through a process the company calls "experimental discovery." In Koch's words, "Given that the market economy is an experimental discovery process, business failures are inevitable and any attempt to eliminate them only ensures overall failure. The key is to recognize when we are experimenting and limit the bet accordingly. . . . Encouraging experimental discovery and not penalizing well-planned experiments that fail fuels an engine of small frequent bets that generates powerful discovery and learning. This is vital to innovation, growth, and long-term profitability."

Create experiments that mitigate risk and provide insights into concept viability. Learn from these experiences while avoiding overanalysis. As an innovation colleague, Ville Keränen, once told me, "One idiot who walks gets further than five intellectuals who only talk."

"Failure is *always* an option. It is the cornerstone of our approach to the scientific method. Any result is a result."—Adam Savage, cohost of television's *MythBusters*

TIP 25

View the World Through
a Different Lens

Be honest. There is something about yourself that you would like to change. Maybe you think you are unattractive, overweight, unintelligent, or unlucky. Regardless of what it is, when you view the world through that lens, that is how the world will be for you. It doesn't matter what evidence you receive to the contrary, because you will still skillfully refute it. If you think you are unattractive and someone pays you a compliment, you will assume that they want something, or that they feel bad for you, or that there must be something wrong with them. We look for and listen to only the evidence that supports our beliefs. Psychologists call this "confirmation bias."

The same holds true for innovation. When you view the world through the lens that your new idea is a good one, you see only the evidence that supports your conclusion, while subconsciously ignoring all of the points that don't. In the process, you might be making some bad innovation investments.

CONFIRMATION BIAS

Confirmation bias is one reason that individuals representing different "sides" of an argument (including politics) honestly feel they have the better argument. It is natural to focus on the strengths of our side and the weaknesses of the other side.

This concept is important to the innovation process and the manner in which you measure your innovation strategies, capabilities, and successes and failures.

Whenever you have an idea, it is human nature for you to search for all of the data that support your belief. You want to prove your concept right and continue to build the case supporting your belief. But in the process you may be ignoring all of the signs that disprove your theory. This can have negative consequences for the organization. Once you believe that your idea is good, it will be difficult for anyone to prove you wrong.

Scott Cook, CEO of Intuit, once wisely said, "For every one of our failures, we had spreadsheets that looked awesome."

For most of your failures, you probably had a lot of evidence for why they were great ideas. However, there was probably also a lot of evidence that did not support your ideas; you just never looked for it.

Make sure that as you develop new concepts and measure their effectiveness, you look for disproving data. Find all of the evidence that refutes your beliefs and hypothesis. This is the first step toward eliminating confirmation bias.

Researchers Martin A. Tolcott and F. Freeman Marvin gave trained U.S. Army intelligence analysts a battlefield scenario.

The analysts were then asked to determine the enemy's most likely avenue of approach and state the level of confidence they had in this analysis. Later, they were given three updated intelligence reports, each of which contained some items that supported their hypotheses and others that disproved them. They were then asked to rate each information item in terms of the degree to which it supported or contradicted their hypothesis.

What the researchers found was that analysts held on to their initial hypotheses. Even though there was significant evidence that disproved their beliefs, the new information somehow increased their confidence levels.

Tolcott and Marvin ran the test again with the same participants. But before doing so, they showed participants how confirmation bias had impacted their decision making the first time around. During the second trial, the participants were given visual reminders designed to help foster their awareness of alternative hypotheses. The result? In general there was a "lower level of confidence, greater consideration of alternative enemy courses of action, and more willingness to reverse early decisions based on new evidence." In fact, during the second trial, 50 percent of the participating teams changed their hypothesis at least once during the exercise.

It is human nature to believe what we want to believe. When we get an idea in our heads, we subconsciously focus our energies on proving that belief right. But being right can be the enemy of good innovation. As an innovator, don't get too attached to your ideas. Proactively play devil's advocate and look for disproving data that will help you measure your innovations against the alternatives, and give that data equal or greater weight. This will allow you to make better decisions on which innovations to pursue and which ones to kill.

As an innovator, don't get too attached to your ideas. Being right can be the enemy of good innovation.

Organization, Leadership, and Culture

Is your organization a cult? In other words, is your culture so strong that it encourages everyone to think the same way? Maybe it's time to hire people who don't "fit the mold." In fact, it may even be time for you to turn your organization upside down. Give up central control and embed innovation in every crevice. Innovation is for the people and by the people. When you treat your employees as owners of the business, you will find that they take the initiative to innovate.

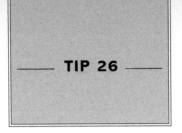

Hire People You Don't Like

I remember a project I worked on many years ago. I was leading a large team and had a very generous budget. I chose John to colead with me because we got along so well. I am a creative, spontaneous, and enthusiastic person, and John was pretty much the same. The team loved working with us. We were fun, engaging, and motivating.

The project was a colossal failure and huge waste of money.

The problem was that John and I got caught up in the novelty of our work. We were too focused on developing new ideas and making sure people were happy. We never got any real work done.

In hindsight, this failure probably could have been predicted. Our working styles were just too similar.

In fact, if you look at any group of people who work effortlessly together, odds are the individuals share a lot in common with one another. They might have similar backgrounds, expertise, interests, or personalities. It's only natural.

The reason? Contrary to "conventional wisdom," opposites do *not* attract.

While individuals who are different from you might initially seem intriguing, in the long run these differences will invariably push you apart. This is a scientifically proven fact. If opposites attracted, our political system would not be the mess it is and we would have Democrats and Republicans hugging and appreciating one another.

The fact is, opposites don't attract. They repel.

What implications does this have on business success?

Think about the people you surround yourself with at work. Are they like you? Do they think the same way? Do they have similar interests, skills, and strengths? Probably.

As a result, teams that lack diversity are the norm.

This desire for similarity has inherent advantages. When people think the same way, act the same way, speak the same way, and use the same language, things get done more quickly.

But is this ultimately good for the business?

To answer this question, consider the research of Clint Bowers and two of his colleagues at the University of Central Florida. They studied how the homogeneity of personalities within work groups affected performance by combining the results of thirteen studies involving five hundred teams.

At first glance, there wasn't much difference in the performance of diverse teams compared to homogeneous teams. But that wasn't the whole story. The types of tasks the teams had to perform had a significant impact on performance.

Bowers and his colleagues went even further and distinguished "low-difficulty" tasks from "high-difficulty" tasks based on how much the activities involved uncertainty, complexity, and demand for high-level processing.

For relatively simple tasks, homogeneous teams consistently

performed more efficiently than heterogeneous ones. When you are surrounded by a bunch of "yes-men" and "yes-women," you agree quickly and get things done.

However, according to Bowers and his team, in situations involving high-difficulty tasks, diverse groups consistently performed more effectively. That is, people who thought differently could innovate better as a group.

This makes sense if you really think about it. Developing something new requires a wide range of thinking. Innovation demands diversity of perspectives, disciplines, and personalities. Having a group of people who think the same way only gives you more of the same. Having people on your team who get along well may seem easier, but it will rarely lead to new and innovative ideas.

Instead, consider the mantra "The person you like the least is the person you need the most."

Someone who is different from you may at times seem annoying. But consider that this person is quite complementary to you. They have skills and perspectives that could provide balance and help you become more effective and innovative. They will challenge you, a crucial factor in business success.

If you only hire people who "fit the mold," you will most likely hit a growth plateau at some point. If you are looking to create a culture of innovation within your organization, first take stock of your current portfolio of people. Do you have a diverse mix of personality styles and divergent perspectives, or do you have a collection of like-minded professionals who will eventually limit the scope of your innovation capabilities?

If your business is creative in nature (e.g., branding or advertising), make sure you hire those with a talent for planning and managing. If your business is operational in nature (e.g., manufacturing), ensure that you have people who are focused on innovation and growth.

People will naturally gravitate toward roles that fit their personality style. Look broadly across your organization. Are there varying styles that exist overall but are siloed within different functional areas? Is your human resources department filled with empathetic communicators? Is your R&D department brimming with analytical and exacting individuals? Look for ways to cross-pollinate these groups to infuse innovation at all levels.

Additionally, consider "hiring in pairs." When at Nissan Design International, Jerry Hirshberg would hire a free-form thinker along with someone who was more analytical. This helped ensure team diversity and the rise of uniquely creative solutions to the company's most pressing problems.

Team diversity is of extreme importance, even within your leadership ranks. When Sigal Barsade and colleagues at the University of Pennsylvania's Wharton business school studied top management teams at large corporations in the United States, they found that the more diverse the functional roles of the team members, the greater the average, market-adjusted financial return in those companies.

Creativity and innovation come from tension, giving rise to differing viewpoints and alternative ways of solving problems. While it may not come naturally, if you want to differentiate yourself from the competition, consider differentiating your perspective by surrounding yourself with people who think differently from how you do.

See appendix B for a simple personality test that will help you identify the right people for your innovation team.

The person you like the least is the person you need the most.

Why the Pyramids Are One
of the Seven Wonders

Most companies start their innovation efforts by creating a new corporate function charged with delivering innovation. These functions are composed of employees who are reassigned to and dedicated to this new organization within the company. In most cases, this is a complete waste of time and money. This model keeps innovation separate from the rest of the business, and there is no involvement by the people who make the important decisions. Additionally, the innovation efforts remain out of touch with the real needs of the business.

Recognizing this common dilemma, USAA, a 22,600-employee financial service firm, took a completely different approach.

At USAA, innovation starts at the leadership level. Leadership sets the tone for the rest of the organization and is a strong advocate for innovative thinking.

Next, USAA created a "core team" composed of thirty-five individuals, all of whom dedicate 100 percent of their time to innovation. However, here is the twist: Only ten of those individuals report directly to the innovation leadership. The other twenty-five "matrixed" individuals spend their time solely on innovation-related activities, yet with a focus on the specific innovation needs of their line of business. This creates widespread buy-in.

What USAA realized was that thirty-five people could not change the culture of a 22,600-person organization. Therefore, beyond the core team, it created a network of two hundred "innovation advisers," each of whom spends 10 percent of their time on innovation efforts, working closely with the core team. In addition, there are ten "innovation champions." These are leaders who serve as powerful advocates for innovation and help break through any challenges that might pop.

How can you use this same method to accelerate your innovation efforts?

First, make sure your leadership team is on board, as they will set the tone, demonstrate strong executive support, and help challenge the status quo.

Of course, your leadership cannot create a culture of innovation on their own, as they have far too many other responsibilities.

Therefore, most organizations tag someone as a full-time "innovation leader" whose role is to help shepherd the innovation process. Innovation leaders are different from other leaders within the organization in that they do not have direct authority over those who make innovation a reality. Ultimately, everyone in the company plays an important role in driving innovation. The innovation leader is more of a mentor, coach, and negotiator than a boss or taskmaster. Their ability to influence and sell the value of innovation and its practices is paramount to their and the organization's success.

Next, create your innovation "core team" (sometimes referred to as a center of excellence), a small cadre of people dedicated to driving innovation into every corner of your organization. In smaller companies made up of few geographies or lines of business, this can indeed be a small central group. But in larger, more widely distributed organizations, the matrixed strategy is preferred, as it addresses the complexities associated with geographic, product, and customer differences.

This core team has many responsibilities. Some of them involve the basics: generating awareness, building the necessary infrastructure, selecting tools, creating training materials and plans, and developing a process for managing the innovation pipeline. But their more valuable role is serving as the eyes and ears of your innovation efforts, providing insights into the specific needs of their departments, employees, customers, vendors, and other stakeholders. They serve as advocates and mentors for innovation, bringing innovation to the masses. They are typically responsible for the development and delivery of innovation/creativity training. They also run brainstorming sessions for various departments. And they play an important role in identifying and shepherding challenges that may exist inside the organization. In essence, they are the go-to people when innovation is needed.

But no core team alone can ever make innovation pervasive. The next step is to pull together your ambassador network. Although all of these individuals are deployed to the lines of business, they must be passionate about innovation. Quite often, these people may dedicate as much as six hours per week (15 percent of their time) to innovation activities. This helps spread the innovation message even deeper into the organization. Since these individuals play such a critical role, contribution to innovation should be one of their performance measures.

How large should your ambassador network be? According to studies conducted by scientist Robin Dunbar, individuals have the capacity to maintain stable relationships with around 150 people. If we use this capacity as a baseline for determining a maximum sphere of influence, having one person in your network for every 150 people you wish to impact (or 0.07 percent) would be appropriate, but 1 percent is a good rule of thumb. At USAA, between the core team and the innovation advisers, almost exactly 1 percent of the organization is represented.

At USAA this approach has worked incredibly well. In only one year, the company achieved 84 percent employee participation and implemented approximately one hundred employee solutions. What were the bottom-line results? There was more than ten times ROI for USAA and almost thirty times ROI for USAA members. USAA is different from shareholder companies in that it has a higher goal and motivation for taking care of its members—present and former members of the military services and their families.

These are impressive results. Follow USAA's lead by embedding innovation throughout the organization.

The Egyptian pyramids worked so well because the majority of the weight was closer to the ground, making these structures more stable. Equally, this pyramid approach to innovation will ground your innovation efforts and fulfill the needs of the business and your customers.

> Everyone in the company plays a role in driving innovation.

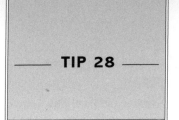

TIP 28

The "Top-Down" Philosophy
Should Be Left to Convertibles

Charles Koch, CEO of Koch Industries, one of the most successful companies in the world, believes that central control is a
"fatal conceit" for organizations. For the past fifty years, Koch
has continually chipped away at the command-and-control style
of management. In its place he asks employees to run their businesses as if they owned them. When someone is brought in
specially to do a job, he or she is immediately given the authority to spend money and to move people when and where he or
she chooses. Decision making within Koch is decentralized as
far as possible to those with the best local knowledge and information. This approach must be working, as Koch Industries has
grown more than 2,200-fold since 1960 and is outperforming
the S&P 500 by nearly 3,200 percent.

Koch Industries is involved in many hazardous businesses,
like asphalt, paper, pulp, oil, and gas. Therefore, a number of
years ago, not satisfied with industry-average accident and in-
jury rates, it set a goal of moving to the top tier in the industry.
Instead of having a few safety engineers scout the company for
unsafe conditions, it made safety the responsibility of each and

every employee. Employees were given rewards both for uncovering unsafe conditions and for discovering new ways to conduct business more safely. This initiative resulted in 35 percent to 50 percent improvements each year in the number and severity of accidents across the company. Within one year the company had moved from the middle of the pack to one of the best safety records in its industry.

This simple example illustrates the value of moving decision making from the top down to the individuals who have the best information and ability to execute. One way of making your organization more innovative is to make sure that it is structured in a way that avoids central control. In fact, this concept of pushing decision making to the lowest levels of the organization is somewhat in vogue at the moment.

One organization that is seeking to spread this business model around the globe is WorldBlu. Traci Fenton, the founder and CEO, calls it "organizational democracy." But unlike most traditional democracies, which conjure up thoughts of politics, bureaucracies, and a "majority rules" mentality, organizational democracy is about giving employees a voice. It is about creating the optimal conditions for learning, motivation, self-direction, and engagement.

Each year, Fenton publishes her "WorldBlu List of Most Democratic Workplaces" in the *New York Times*. In it you will find some interesting examples of democracy in action.

At GE/Durham, where jet engines are assembled, almost all decisions are made in consensus by teams. Whole Foods uses an open "salary book" that lists the previous year's salary and bonus for every employee by name. Semco allows employees to choose both their boss and how much they get paid. W. L. Gore has what it calls a "flat lattice" approach instead of layers of hierarchy so that there is no chain of command and the employees have direct connections to whomever they need.

Another example that Fenton shares comes from Colorado-based DaVita. With over 32,000 employees, this company provides dialysis treatments to patients suffering from chronic kidney failure. But back in 1999, the company was on the verge of bankruptcy. The new CEO, Kent Thiry, decided that major changes were needed. How did he do it? Rather than centralizing control in Denver, management made the radical choice of decentralizing power to the company's 1,500 clinics nationwide. By providing a clear set of parameters and then giving each clinic the freedom to be its own boss within those boundaries, Thiry communicated a message of trust and respect to all the employees. Decisions are made either by consensus or by a majority vote. Every decision doesn't need to go before the entire company. Instead, those who have the best information to make decisions should make them (and that doesn't usually include the people at the top). Each quarter, DaVita teammates are invited to participate in a "Voice of the Village" call with the CEO and the senior leadership team. The call allows employees to share information about the state of the company and address any areas of concern.

The results of these efforts? Operating revenues grew from $1.45 billion in 1999 to $6.1 billion in 2009, and the following year the company made the *Fortune* 400.

Innovation does not always involve new products or services. Instead, innovation can be used to help reshape your business.

Innovation will organically emerge once you treat your employees as owners of the business. Although it may feel safer to control every decision, you may just control yourself out of business.

> Central control is a fatal conceit. You may just control yourself out of business.

TIP 29

Use the Reality TV Show Model

The Quill Corporation (a subsidiary of Staples) used a creative approach to introduce challenge-driven innovation within its organization. Using *The Apprentice* as a model, the company launched an internal competition called "The Quillionaire" in which three teams of eight people competed against one another each month. These teams were focused on solving specific business challenges, and this approach encouraged collaboration within the teams, yet made for some friendly competition.

After a month, each team presented its solutions to a panel of judges composed of four executives. The judges' role was to encourage participants while still challenging their solutions. The teams developed creative solutions—some of which were implemented. Everyone had a great time, and each month the winning team had dinner with the president at a restaurant of their choosing.

In addition to being fun, because the competitions were organized around a specific challenge, they served as a catalyst for rolling out larger challenge-driven initiatives within the organization. The competitions were also videotaped in front of a live audience and used for internal marketing purposes.

This is one example of how a reality television show can be

used to help drive innovation. These competitions are different from the "tournaments" discussed in tip 10. These are done with employees and are as much about generating buzz and stimulating interest in innovation as they are about finding specific solutions. One side benefit of these types of competitions is that they take the pressure off "getting things right" and add some fun to the workplace. As a result, you might find solutions that are out of the ordinary.

Given the success of the Quillionaire competition, several years later, as part of its ongoing innovation efforts, Quill reintroduced the reality TV show–like concept by launching its "The BIGGEST Winner!" contest. A total of 220 individuals submitted 139 ideas, which were judged by a panel of Quill executives. They reviewed employee ideas in a two-stage process, beginning with an essay and expanding into a detailed executive summary along with visual presentations. Ideas were judged on their value proposition, competitive advantage, feasibility and risk, market potential/resources, and uniqueness/originality of concept.

Although this was more akin to the *American Idol* approach, the competition resulted in a junior staff member modeling a program that had the potential to create a nine-million-dollar revenue stream for Quill, a sizable amount for a one-billion-dollar company. To ensure the solution's success, the company promoted the contributor, and a vice president was assigned to mentor her as she worked to make sure the idea took hold.

In these two examples, a select panel of executives determined the winners. In another instance, the competitors' peers made the final decision. A well-known electronics company holds a "county fair" each year. A huge room is set up with hundreds of booths, and all employees are encouraged to have their own booths to present new ideas. Ideas can be on anything—not necessarily even from the employee's section of the business. In the end, the employees vote on the winners. This competition is much more about pride than about prize. To be selected by a group of one's peers is quite an honor.

Although the county fair is akin to using an idea-driven approach, it requires everyone to put time and effort into fleshing out a concept and creating a physical prototype. This requires the developer to think more deeply about the concept and often leads to better results. Although people have to dedicate their own time to producing stellar ideas, they are happy to do it because it taps into their true passions. As a result, it both demonstrates a greater commitment to the idea's success and encourages a more engaging process than simple virtual electronic suggestion boxes.

The Apprentice, The Biggest Loser, or *American Idol.* It doesn't matter which show you choose. The point is to identify ways for infusing fun, competition, and peer engagement that has your organization focused on specific and meaningful challenges. When you run these competitions, everyone comes out a winner.

> These competitions are as much about generating buzz and stimulating interest in innovation as they are about finding specific solutions.

Get Your Knowledge Workers Doing Knowledge Work

At the start of my career I worked for a large computer manu-facturer. On average, I worked fifty hours a week. My direct supervisor worked sixty hours a week. Life was good, until my supervisor was laid off and I inherited all of her work. Faced with having to work 110 hours a week, I decided to take a hard look at what we were doing. What I discovered is what many organizations would discover if they took the time to do the same type of analysis: Only a small percentage of employees' time is spent on truly valuable work.

Time is a precious commodity inside organizations. There are barely enough hours in the day to do your regular job, let alone innovate on the side. How do you make time when you have none? The key to making time is to eliminate the unnecessary. Although this may seem obvious, it is rarely done in most orga-nizations.

Over the course of a weekend, I analyzed all of the activities I was expected to perform. I hoped to get my work from 110 hours to 50 hours (or less). Here's what I found.

Only 20 percent of my work was high value-add. These were the high-priority items I still needed to perform.

Many activities added no value. Although we had done these activities in the past, they were no longer necessary. I stopped doing these immediately, and no one seemed to notice.

Several activities were really the responsibility of another department or individual. Therefore, I worked to get these activities assigned to the correct parties. Not only did this reduce my workload, but it also reduced the overall time required by the company as a whole. It is always more efficient for the right person to do the right work.

Additionally, a large number of "transactional" activities were done manually and were candidates for automation. None of these activities was particularly complicated. Therefore, I wrote some simple computer programs in a matter of hours that automated these processes.

After only two days of analysis and work, I managed to get my workload from 110 hours to 20 hours. The point wasn't to reduce my workload. It was to make sure that I and others focused our energies on the activities that would have the greatest impact.

One way to make time is to get your knowledge workers doing knowledge work. For example, consider a valuable resource in most organizations: the sales representative. On average (based on my own studies), these valuable workers spend an appalling 20 percent to 35 percent of their time face-to-face with customers. The rest of the time is spent traveling, filling out forms, and sitting in meetings. This is an example of knowledge workers spending little time on valuable knowledge work.

Imagine if you increased the level of knowledge work from 25 percent to 50 percent. You would, in essence, double your workforce without hiring a single person.

One notably bad example comes from a food company. Brand managers, particularly important in the food business, were spending less than 30 percent of their time on brand management, while the rest of their time went to administration, meetings, and bureaucracy.

One of the keys to helping knowledge workers focus on high-value tasks is to off-load transactional, repetitive, and administrative tasks to others (whether customers, clerks, computers, or outsourcing companies). The greatest value of technology and outsourcing is its ability to leverage an organization's assets and allow people to do more valuable work.

As another example, at the social services department in Merced County, California, most of the employees are social workers. Nevertheless, in the past they spent almost none of their time on social work. They were busy with administrative tasks such as entering claims forms and searching manual records. Now, new systems help automate that work, freeing the social workers to do the job they were hired to do. Their overall ability to deliver services has improved significantly.

Here are a few simple strategies for making more time in your day:

- What work is non-value-add? Stop doing it!
- What work do you do that others *should* do? Reassign that work to the appropriate party who has the best skills and authority. This will help get the work done more efficiently.

- What work do you do that others *can* do? If you are a knowledge worker, delegate or outsource your less important activities. This will free time to focus on what matters most.
- What work can be automated? Buy off-the-shelf software to help speed things up, or find someone who can build you a custom solution.

Innovation is recognized by most companies as a basic requirement for ensuring business sustainability. Cliché as it may be, it is time to "work smarter, not harder." Focus your energies on the items that are truly value-add and differentiate you from the competition. Eliminate, automate, or delegate the rest.

> One way to make time is to get your knowledge workers doing knowledge work.

CREATIVITY

Techniques for Stimulating Creative Thinking

Innovation is an end-to-end process. Generating solutions is one of the steps in that process that requires creative thinking. To make innovation a reality, you need employees who think differently. This section contains a number of tips and techniques that can pump up their creative potential.

Encourage Employees to
Get on Their Soapbox

I lived in London for several years and loved visiting Hyde Park's "Speaker's Corner" on Sundays. In this corner of the park, people can speak on any topic, typically about politics, religion, conspiracy theories, or alien abductions. The most compelling individuals draw a crowd. People who are less interesting usually end up taking their soapbox home early in the day.

This is a free market in action. The best speakers, as judged by the listeners, thrive, while others fade away. Watching this, I realized that the Speaker's Corner concept could be a useful technique for driving new thinking.

Think about your typical brainstorming session. Usually there is one person facilitating the conversation. To overcome the unproductive nature of these conversations, some groups break up into smaller groups. The problem with this approach is that it does not allow for cross-pollination of ideas, as people are sequestered at different tables or in different rooms.

To combat these problems, try emulating the Speaker's Corner approach. Instead of one conversation, there are many. Instead of the leader deciding what to discuss, everyone determines what is important. And people can participate in multiple conversations.

Here's how it works.

- Capture (either in the meeting or in advance) a list of topics that are of interest to the individuals in the room. These can be based on preference or they can be based on a predefined list of challenges, ideas, or solutions that are important to the organization.
- Prioritize this list down to a critical few issues. The ideal number is one topic for every eight people. For the sake of argument, let's say there are thirty people participating; you would have four topics/corners.
- Ask for volunteers—one for each topic/corner—who agree to facilitate that particular conversation. Each facilitator goes to a different "corner" with a flip chart to capture the conversations associated with their assigned topic.
- Meeting attendees can then wander freely from corner to corner as they see fit. The only rule is that everyone must either be adding value to a corner or receiving value from a corner. If not, they should go to a different corner or create a new corner.
- Any person, at any time, can create a new corner around any topic. The new topic can be from the list, it can be an extension of an existing corner, or it can be a new topic altogether.
- Should a corner leader wish to participate in another discussion, they can recruit a new leader to continue with their topic.

What you will find is that the most important topics with the highest level of energy attract the most people. Topics that fail to attract a crowd wither on the vine (just as in Hyde Park—time to pick up the soapbox and call it a day). In one hour, you can capture more ideas than you would from a day full of meetings, and each topic benefits from the cross-pollination of ideas from all attendees.

As an example, before a Speaker's Corner session with fifty participants, a client conducted a survey to determine the most pressing issues and concerns of the employees. Based on responses, it chose the most popular six topics. During the event, when people were given the opportunity to choose which corner to go to, over thirty people wanted to talk about workforce productivity. We had clearly underestimated how much interest there would be in this topic, so we took a few minutes to break the subject into subtopics, creating two additional yet slightly different corners focused on productivity. Two of the original six corners didn't attract anyone and were quickly shut down. The other conversations continued for about ninety minutes until all topics were addressed fully by all interested participants.

The Speaker's Corner approach allows participants to discuss what they are most passionate about. Hot topics attract a crowd, while the less popular ones are shut down. Innovate the way your employees brainstorm and you'll see an immediate difference in the quality and quantity of their conversations.

The Speaker's Corner concept is a useful technique for driving new thinking. It is a free market in action.

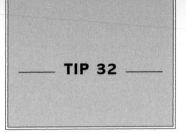

TIP 32

The Shortest Distance Between
Two Points Is a Straight Line

In a recent client session, I had everyone in the room get into groups of two. I then pulled a brick from my briefcase and we proceeded to do the following activity:

I said, "In your pairs, I want you to go back and forth and develop a list of all of the different ways in which you could use a brick. The first person might say, 'Put the brick under the wheels of a car to prevent it from rolling backward.' The second person might say, 'Put the brick in the toilet's tank to reduce the amount of water that is used while flushing.' Then the first person might say, 'Use the brick as a replacement for the remote control when you can't find it. Throw it at the TV to turn it off.' The quality of the ideas doesn't matter. Just think freely. You have one minute to develop solutions."

The responses ranged from using it as a paperweight to a bookend to a weapon.

In general, people developed their solutions by looking at the brick and considering its physical attributes: rough, heavy, and potentially dangerous. (See graphic at top of the next page.) When I polled the groups for their answers, I found that most

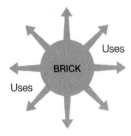

people had developed very similar solutions and that the range of creativity was limited.

We then played a second round.

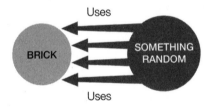

"The question is the same," I said. "What are all of the different ways in which you can use a brick? But this time, instead of looking at the physical attributes of the brick, I want you to think of something random and find ways of using a brick in that situation."

"For example," I continued, "if the random item was 'the body,' think of all the ways of using a brick on the body. You could use it as a weight to build up your biceps. You could use it as a loofah to slough off dead skin cells. You could balance it on your head to improve your posture. Or a short guy like me could attach it to the bottom of his shoes to increase his height.

"The first person in your pair will name something random. The second person will then take one minute to develop as many possible uses for a brick in that random context. Then you will switch, and the second person will name something random and the first person will create a list of uses."

The difference in results was staggering. This time there was a much greater variety of solutions generated.

I have polled audiences around the world to see which approach, in their opinion, led to solutions that were more creative. Consistently, between 75 percent and 95 percent of audience members choose the second method—connect to something random—which I describe as "line thinking." I describe the first method as "dot thinking": looking at the attributes of the brick/problem and generating solutions from there.

Why do most people select the second method? Maybe it is because "line thinking" represents the true essence of creativity. Or as Steve Jobs once said, "Creativity is just having enough dots to connect." The key word being "connect."

How do you use this concept to develop new solutions?

Choose a random object. When you think of or look at this object, what solutions come to mind? What are the characteristics of this object? How can these characteristics help you solve a problem?

Where can you get ideas that stimulate this process?

- *Trends*—Identify trends and then force associations. Associations are line thinking in action. Look at industry-specific trends and more general trends. For example, how can an aging population give you an idea for a new product or service?

- *Words, expressions, and idioms*—Use a dictionary, phrase book, or quotation guide. Select a random word and see how it might stimulate a new solution.
- *Magazines*—Get a bunch of magazines that are not associated with your business. Then rip out pictures, headlines, or anything that attracts your attention. Force associations and be sure to find real, tangible solutions rather than fluffy platitudes.
- *Look around*—Look around the room and force associations with random items you see.

The key is to become masterful at connecting the dots.

The next few techniques are variations on the brick exercise and are designed to help develop new solutions or new applications of existing solutions.

Both ways of thinking—dot and line thinking—are valid and useful problem-solving approaches. In fact, both are necessary. Dot thinking tends to lead to incremental-improvement ideas that are critical to any business for day-to-day operations, short-term growth, and traditional problem solving. However, when you are looking for more radical solutions that drive long-term strategic growth, line thinking is the way to go.

> "Creativity is just having enough dots to connect."—Steve Jobs

TIP 33

Someone Else Has Already
Solved Your Problem

Imagine you want to create a waterproof, biodegradable adhesive that is also safe to use inside the body as a way of augmenting sutures or staples. Where would you turn? Consider the possibility that someone else might have already solved this problem. Or in the case of the medical adhesive, *something* has already solved this problem. By studying the gecko lizard's "gravity-defying feet," researchers have been able to develop a new type of medical adhesive with these exact properties.

The best way to quickly find solutions to your challenges is to identify someone who has already solved the problem—but in a different context. That is, someone from another industry, discipline, or practice might have a solution.

Previously I mentioned how a toothpaste manufacturer developed a novel concept for whitening teeth by using the same blueing agents that are used in laundry detergent to whiten clothes.

Another toothpaste innovation comes from GlaxoSmith-Kline. Its "Aquafresh iso-active" toothpaste is based on an idea from a GSK cleaning product that is a gel but foams upon use, much like gel shaving creams. The toothpaste comes out like a gel but foams in the mouth. This formulation removes 25 percent more bacteria than regular toothpaste and has proven to be a market success.

All of this research about toothpaste got me thinking. If toothpaste manufacturers can find solutions from shaving cream and laundry detergent, where else could they look? To generate new concepts, I selected a few items from my house to "connect" with toothpaste:

1. *Pop Rocks:* Pop Rocks is a carbonated candy that explodes in your mouth. What if you added Pop Rock–like crystals to toothpaste? Not only would the toothpaste foam, but it would also fizz and explode and possibly blast the plaque off your teeth.

2. *Shampoo:* Shampoos are infused with vitamins and minerals. What if you infused toothpaste with these ingredients on top of fluoride? Or maybe you could add some homeopathic remedies. Sublingual administration (under the tongue) is a common and effective way of delivering drugs directly into the bloodstream and might prove useful for those who don't like taking pills.

3. *Conditioner:* We use shampoo to clean and conditioner to protect. What if they created a tooth conditioner, a special toothpaste that you use after your regular toothpaste? It could coat your teeth to prevent staining, bad breath, or split ends. What if you created a "leave-in" conditioner, a toothpaste that is applied but not spit out and could keep on working all day long? Even better, they could borrow the "technology"

used by shampoos like Pert Plus, which combine shampoo and conditioner into one formulation.

4. *Moisturizers:* Several moisturizers have an A.M. and a P.M. formulation. One is used in the morning and the other at night before you go to sleep. The A.M. formula of toothpaste could be infused with caffeine that would be absorbed into the bloodstream sublingually. And the P.M. formulation could be infused with melatonin to help you sleep better at night.

5. *Weight-Loss Products:* What if you could create toothpaste that reacted with certain unhealthy foods, making them taste bad? This might cause you to reduce the amount of food you eat. Or what if you created a toothpaste with an appetite suppressant?

Of course, the ultimate answer might involve a product that eliminates the need for brushing altogether.

The purpose of this exercise is to bring us to one of the most useful questions in the world of creativity: "Who else has solved this problem?"

When you ask this question, you may quickly find a solution to your challenge. To find solutions from other industries, processes, products, or disciplines, ask the following questions:

- What is the problem you want to solve (e.g., How do we make teeth whiter without abrasives or bleaches?)?
- What is a more "abstract" way to frame the problem (e.g., How do we make something that is already white even whiter?)?
- Who else is addressing a similar problem (e.g., laundry detergents that use blueing agents)?

- How could you adapt their solution to your problem (e.g., create a toothpaste with a blue dye in the middle)?

How has this concept been used in the real world?

A gas pipeline company developed a new technology for finding and sealing pipeline cracks by mirroring the clotting agents in the human body.

A boat rental company uses a Netflix-like subscription model. Netflix allows you to receive an unlimited number of DVDs each month, but you can only have a certain number (depending on your subscription level) in your possession at any given time. A boat company gives members unlimited access to a number of boats with two open reservation slots at any given time. As soon as you use one reservation, you get another.

A company wanted to find a better way of diagnosing computer crashes. It wanted the ability to replay the crash so that it could re-create the problem. Who has solved this? TiVo—the digital video recorder. The idea was devised when the inventor Jonathan Lindo asked the question "Wouldn't it be great if we could just TiVo this and replay it?" As a result, ReplayDIRECTOR was created to record all of your activities, enabling you to replay them later to help diagnose computer crashes, much like TiVo.

Solutions can come from anywhere.

Sometimes the best solutions already exist inside your own organization. In innovation parlance, the sharing of ideas across business units and brands is referred to as "convergence." For many organizations, such as Johnson & Johnson, this is one of the most critical components of their innovation program. You just need to frame the question properly in order to be able to identify the most appropriate product line, function, division, or brand where this problem has already been solved.

And of course, in some cases the best solutions will come from outside your company or even outside the world of business.

Where will your next big innovation come from?

> The most useful question in the world of creativity: "Who else has solved this problem?"

TIP 34

Adapt Your Product to a
Different Environment

Although label maker manufacturers sell their products primarily through office supply stores, the products' uses are unlimited. One such manufacturer, in an effort to expand its reach, made a list of two hundred different possible customer segments: hospitals, authors, farmers, computer technicians, tollbooth collectors, or hotel concierges. Then each day the manufacturer would choose one from the list and develop a list of possible marketing opportunities. Although sometimes a slight product adaptation was needed, in many cases it was simply a matter of changing the marketing materials.

The previous tips were about creating new products. But sometimes the best innovation is about taking something that already exists and adapting it for a new environment. How might you sell your products/services to a totally different customer market than you normally do? Make a random list of potential targets and "force" an association between your existing product and that market's needs. Then find ways of marketing and packaging your product to meet those needs.

How can you take a product that has no market potential and

turn it into a cash cow? Consider Arm & Hammer. Baking soda is a commodity. And because few people bake from scratch anymore, getting people to buy more baking soda for baking is a losing proposition. What do you do? Find new uses. Arm & Hammer turned its simple baking soda into an empire of product extensions. Refrigerator fresheners made of 100 percent baking soda, supported with clever packaging. Carpet fresheners made of nearly 100 percent baking soda, enhanced with a mild fragrance. Laundry wash booster, toothpaste, pot and pan cleaners, polishes, and more. The company took a simple product and extended it in previously unimaginable ways.

Although it is not always advisable to stray too far from your core audience or product, adaptive innovation can sometimes provide an extra revenue boost without your needing to invest heavily in new products.

> Sometimes the best innovation is about taking something that already exists and adapting it for a new environment.

Don't Put the "No" in InNOvation

Improvisational comedy is a great creativity training tool. The great improv comedian Neil Mullarkey (yes, that's his real name) once taught me an improvisational game called "yeah, but." The objective is to tell a story, one person at a time, without using the words "yeah, but."

This is relevant to innovation, because so many people put the "no" in inNOvation. New ideas are often met with the immediate response, "Yeah, but," followed by a dozen reasons why the idea won't work—we don't have enough money, there is not enough time, it's good for someone else but not for us. Instead, use "Yes, and." This is an improv comedy technique where you build on the ideas of others using the words "Yes, and," while eliminating "Yeah, but" from your vocabulary.

The next time you have a problem to solve, like inventing the next hot design for your product, try this game. Have one person throw out the first idea, and then continue with, "Yes, and . . . ," building on the previous idea. The key is to answer quickly and avoid overthinking. Top-of-head answers tend to tap into a part of the brain we don't use during our normal thinking process. Be sure that your answer is a contribution. It should build on what the previous person said rather than invalidate it. You will develop many new ideas over the course of play. Many of the ideas will be duds. Don't worry! Play with it. Have fun. You never know when you will find a real gem. After all, it is only a game. Over time, this will become a normal mode of operating. You will become the master at breakthrough thinking on a regular basis by building on the ideas of others. As Sir Isaac Newton once said, "If I have seen further it is only by standing on the shoulders of giants."

Of course, while fleshing out ideas, concerns will surface that need to be addressed. You can't just sweep these "yeah, buts" under the rug. In these situations, learn to phrase concerns as challenges. For example, when brainstorming, inevitably someone will say, "We don't have enough time to implement this idea" or "We don't have enough money." Instead, state this concern as a challenge, such as "How might we get more money?" or "How might we do this for less money?" Once you define a new challenge, you can use any of these creativity techniques to find new solutions.

Practice doing this every day. If you struggle with breaking the "yeah, but" mentality, put a jar in your home or office. Any time you or others say, "Yeah, but," put a dollar in the jar to help raise awareness and deter the voicing of these negative reactions to your (and their) ideas. It is a fun, nonthreatening way of providing feedback to your peers. Use the money to take improv training classes.

> In the improvisational game "yeah, but," the objective is to tell a story, one person at a time, without using the words "yeah, but."

How Can You Make the
Impossible Possible?

Magicians are master innovators. They make the impossible possible. They decide, "Hey, I want to slice a woman in half," and then they find a way to do it without killing the subject.

In this, there is a useful lesson for creative thinking.

Sometimes we get stuck in the mundane. We get stuck in thinking about what's real and what's actually possible.

But what if you could become masterful at making the seemingly impossible possible? What if, instead of solving possible challenges, you started to solve seemingly impossible ones? What if, instead of looking for realistic solutions to challenges, you started with solutions that seemed impractical?

When solving problems, we typically attempt to move from point A (where we are today) to point B (where we want to go). But often we fall short and end up still at A' (as depicted in the graphic at the top of the next page).

However, if we shoot for point C (the seemingly impossible), even if we fall short, we might just hit point B.

When solving a problem, a useful question to ask is "What are impossible or impractical solutions?" This question will

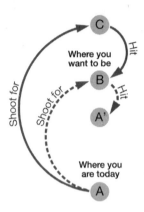

stretch your thinking. From there, you can then figure out ways of making these impractical solutions practical. To encourage this kind of thinking, try this technique. It can be done in pairs or with small groups. It is done in a few simple steps.

STEP 1: As always, make sure you have a clearly defined opportunity/challenge statement. Example: "How might we promote our new Internet-based business?"

STEP 2: Have one person give an outrageous solution. I typically suggest that if it is not "illegal, immoral, or impossible," it is probably not wild enough. Example: "Rearrange the stars in the sky to spell out our Web site address."

STEP 3: Have the other person (or people) list three attributes they like about that solution. Example: (a) Everyone in the world can see it; (b) It is permanent; (c) It doesn't adversely affect the environment.

STEP 4: Next, have the other person (or people) list three things that would make the solution even better. Example: (a) Have it be visible twenty-four hours a day, not just at night; (b) Design it so that you don't have to look up to see it; (c) Create a concept such that people won't have to remember or write down the Web site address.

STEP 5: Finally, use the attributes identified in steps 3 and 4 to either refine the original solution or develop different ones. Examples: Attribute 4(a) (visible twenty-four hours a day) may lead to the Web site address being displayed in lights in Times Square, New York City. Or "twenty-four hours a day" and "stars" might get you thinking about movie stars and how they might promote your business. Or attribute 3(b) (make it permanent) might get you thinking about other permanent things, such as tattoos. What if you created a nicely designed temporary rub-on tattoo? Or got nightclub owners to stamp your Web address on the hands of people as they entered?

This approach works well because step 2 allows you to think without constraints. Step 3 "validates" the original solution and the person who generated it. And steps 4 and 5 make the solution practical.

Instead of just going for what seems practical, shoot for the seemingly impossible . . . and make it possible.

What if you could become masterful at making the seemingly impossible possible? What if, instead of looking for realistic solutions to challenges, you started with solutions that seemed impractical?

Stand in Someone Else's Shoes

Think back to the last time you bought a car. What did you notice as you drove your shiny new vehicle off the lot? Did you notice that everyone else seemed to be driving the same car? Obviously the number of cars like yours on the road did not increase overnight. Instead, by changing the "filter" through which you viewed the world, you changed how it appeared to you.

Because we can only see the world through the filter we have built up over time, the only way to change perspectives is to change the filter. Unfortunately, it is difficult to "see" the filter you are using. Sometimes it is easier to replace your existing filter with a new one.

Try this. Each morning when you wake up, make believe you are someone different. Pretend you are a detective, a mechanic, an artist, or a gardener. It really doesn't matter whom you choose to be. You will then begin to see things over the course of the day that you have never seen before. By focusing on different elements, you will begin to have new experiences and new perspectives.

You can also use this concept more analytically during brainstorming sessions. To do this, use the following steps:

- Identify the person you want to emulate. You can do this randomly. Or you can consider people who are from completely different disciplines and who have solved related problems. What are their primary characteristics? For example, you might choose Walt Disney, who is known for creating magical experiences.
- Next, ask, "How would this person solve this problem?" If you were to hire them as a consultant to your organization, what would they suggest? Disney might encourage you to redesign your customer experience to be more engaging, even when customers are waiting in queue.

Creativity requires us to see the world with fresh eyes. Unfortunately, it is difficult to overcome ingrained perspectives and habitual thinking. By standing in someone else's shoes, we can see the world through their eyes, offering us different vantage points.

> Each morning when you wake up, make believe you are someone different.

TIP 38

Innovation Is Child's Play

I remember once watching two young boys playing outside. They wore bedsheets fashioned into capes. The first boy started by making his fingers into a gun, pointing it the other boy, and saying, "I'm zapping you with my laser beam." The second boy said, "That's okay, because I am wearing my mirrored suit, so the laser is bouncing back at you." And the play continued for hours, going back and forth between the two children until it was time for lunch.

The concept of play and games can be a useful tool for enhancing creativity. They make work more fun, they reduce stress, and they get people involved in the action. However, not all games are created equal. The games adults play are certainly not child's play.

The games adults play tend to have rigid rules, an ending, and winners and losers. Think about it: Monopoly, poker, or basketball. These activities all have a complex set of rules that the players must adhere to. If you break the rules, you "go to jail," are disqualified, or get penalized. And these games have a well-defined end. Play is over when all of the other players are out of money, when everyone has had their turn, or when the "clock" says there's no more time. And nearly every adult game has a winner and one or more losers. They are competitions. Although these games can be fun, they tend to create a focus on winning.

Contrast this with the way kids play. They have very loose rules, they play the game until they say it ends, and there is no concept of winner/loser. Kids make up the rules as they go along. They improvise. Even universal rules don't apply to kids. They can don a cape and fly through the air, defying the laws of gravity. Rarely is a stopwatch involved. Children simply play until they get tired of that game. And then they invent a new game. The only clocks involved with kids' games are the watches on the wrists of their parents.

When children play, there are no winners or losers. Yes, they might have battles with imaginary swords or superpowers. And there are victims who get hurt or die in the heat of battle. But they come back as a new character. The play does not end with the death of a player.

Adult games can limit creativity. The rules, deadlines, and pressure prevent a flow of new ideas. They create stress.

If you want to enhance creativity, passion, and productivity, I encourage you to play like kids. These timeless, unbounded, and rule-free games can create an environment of free-flowing thinking. Studies show that 98 percent of five-year-olds test as highly creative, yet only 2 percent of adults do. We don't lose our creativity; we learn habits that stop it from emerging.

How does this apply to your organization?

I'm not suggesting that you go out and buy a foosball table or Nerf balls. Instead, find ways to stretch the imagination. One way to do this is to view lofty goals as a game rather than as a stress-inducing end goal.

Imagine a company that has a target of doubling its business over the next five years. That equates to a 14 percent growth rate each year (assuming compounding). Most companies, with hard work and some creative thinking, could hit those numbers, although it would certainly not be easy.

Because a 14 percent growth rate is viewed as doable, it might create a certain expectation in the minds of the executives and employees. This is an adult game. It becomes competitive, and you (the individual or the organization) either win or lose.

But what if the organization set a target of growing by 50 percent a year? That level of growth is unprecedented, and it would certainly stretch the way employees think. A 14 percent improvement can most likely be attained through conventional thinking. But a 50 percent growth target would require a breakthrough.

It might also have an interesting psychological impact on the organization. Because a 50 percent growth rate is unheard of, especially for a well-established large corporation, clearly no one in the organization would be expecting that outcome. Surely the top executives would not expect employees to deliver on those targets.

As a result, the 50 percent target becomes a "game." As long as everyone in the organization believes they are playing a game that is designed to energize them and is not specifically designed around hitting the target, they will naturally become more motivated. This, in turn, will stimulate creativity. Even if the company does not hit 50 percent growth rates, it will certainly have a better chance of hitting 14 percent than if it focused on that as the end goal.

In the words of Michelangelo, "The greater danger for most of us is not that our aim is too high and we miss it, but that it is too low and we hit it."

"The greater danger for most of us is not that our aim is too high and we miss it, but that it is too low and we hit it."
—Michelangelo

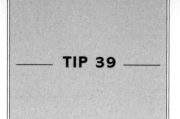

TIP 39

Sometimes It's Logical to Be Illogical

Some of the most creative ideas come from the most unnatural combinations. Imagine a "slot machine" that facilitates illogical combinations of "who, what, where, when, how, and how much" parameters. When you pull the handle, random combinations are generated.

For example, if you are tasked with redesigning the supermarket checkout process, you might look at the "who," "where," and "when" parameters.

- "Who" options might be the cashier, customer, random employee, or no one.
- "Where" options might be the cash register, on the shelf, in the shopping cart, at home, or at the exit.
- "When" options might be while placing item in cart, after making all purchases, or before making purchases.

The typical combination for supermarket checkout is that it is done by the cashier (who), at the cash register (where), after all of the purchases are made (when).

When you spin the wheels of the slot machine, you might get some random combinations like the following:

- *Random Option 1:* The customer (who) scans as they make their purchases (when) on their shopping cart (where). A number of supermarkets now use this checkout system, whereby customers can scan their items as they go with a handheld scanner.
- *Random Option 2:* Scanning is done at the exit (where) by no one (who) after all of the purchases are made. To make this option work, RFID technology could be used so that all of the groceries are scanned via radio frequency as the customer leaves. If the shopper has an RFID tag on their key chain that is linked to a credit card on file, scanning of individual items could be eliminated
- *Random Option 3:* The customer (who) scans at home (where) before making purchases (when). If customers have a scanner attached to their trash can, they can scan the bar code after a product is used when they throw out the empty package. This could trigger an automatic replenishment for home delivery.

You get the idea. The possibilities are endless. Although many combinations may end up being duds, when you get a winner, the payoff can be huge.

And you don't need to build your own slot machine. You can simply make lists of the different options for each parameter and then randomly select one from each column.

WHO	WHEN	WHERE
Cashier	After Purchase	At the Checkout Counter
Customer	Before Purchase	At the Point of Food Pickup
Floor Walker	During Purchase	On the Shopping Cart
Automated Technology	Before Going to the Store	At Another Location
Someone Else	After Leaving the Store	At the Customer's Home
No One	After Using the Product	At the Exit

Using this approach is a great way to uncover implicit assumptions about the business. When you generate combinations that are different from those used in the past, people will almost surely say, "Hey, we can't do that because . . ." You then begin to uncover the underlying assumptions. This is where real creativity can emerge.

Illogical combinations can lead to truly logical solutions.

Illogical combinations can lead to truly logical solutions.

Predict What the Competition Will Do Next

On December 22, 2001, Richard Reid was caught with plastic explosives in the soles of his shoes. That's why we now have to walk barefoot through airports while our shoes are scanned. On August 9, 2006, two dozen people were arrested in the UK because they were plotting to bring liquid explosives onto planes leaving Heathrow Airport. As a result, we now have to travel with miniature shampoos, shaving creams, and toothpastes.

Enron had its meltdown. What was done in response? Stringent rules like the Sarbanes-Oxley Act were implemented. When our financial institutions started to falter, seven hundred billion dollars of the taxpayers' money was spent to sort out the mess.

These are examples of a "reactionary" approach to innovation. Wait for something to happen and then try to devise a response.

Most organizations use creativity to help them determine what to do next based on current information. They brainstorm ideas, select the best solutions, and then implement the most promising ones. Creativity is used to determine what *your organization* will do next.

But in these rapidly changing times, creativity can be even more valuable for determining what the *marketplace and your competitors* will do next. Or, if you are the government, it may help determine what banks and terrorists will do next.

When is the last time you had a brainstorming session where you asked the following questions?

- What are we most afraid our competition will do to us?
- Who is not a competitor now but might be in the future?
- What shift might happen in the buying habits of our customers that might make our product/service less appealing?
- How can the sagging economy help our business?
- What emerging products or services might make our business irrelevant?

The list of outside-in questions can be endless—and valuable. In your next brainstorming session, try the following:

- Brainstorm your own list of questions, building on mine above.
- Determine which ones you want to tackle first.
- Brainstorm, using a variety of creativity techniques, to identify "possible" outcomes.
- For those that are deemed plausible, brainstorm a list of "triggers" for each. These are market conditions that tell you that the given scenario is moving from "possible" to "plausible."
- Set up a corporate "radar" system to help monitor external conditions. Have everything in place such that you can implement critical innovations when market conditions dictate.

This approach blends creativity with scenario-based planning. It helps you move from reactive solutions to proactive solutions. And in today's volatile world, this might just be the key to your long-term survival.

> In these rapidly changing times, creativity can be even more valuable for determining what the *marketplace and your competitors* will do next.

APPENDIX A:

TECHNOLOGIES THAT ENABLE INNOVATION

Up to this point, this book has contained tips on how to leverage your innovation process, strategy, people, and measures. However, in today's fast-paced world, technology has become an important enabler of the entire innovation process, and a number of software platforms exist to help facilitate this.

Functionality varies from platform to platform. Some of these software products allow management to define specific challenges and then look for solutions, while others are particularly useful for gathering ideas and customer insights. Some tools enable voting and evaluation, while others use more sophisticated "predictive markets." And some are best for internal collaboration, while others are optimized for external crowdsourcing.

Each tool has its own strengths and associated limitations.

Here are a few players in the collaborative innovation space (in alphabetical order):

- Brightidea (www.brightidea.com)
- Hype (www.hypeinnovation.com)
- Imaginatik (www.imaginatik.com)
- InnoCentive (www.innocentive.com)
- Jive (www.jivesoftware.com)

- Salesforce's "Ideas" (www.salesforce.com/crm/customer-service-support/ideation)
- Spigit (www.spigit.com)

Other products exist that serve different purposes. For example, Invention Machine's Goldfire (www.inventionmachine.com) helps automate common innovation tasks, while ThoughtOffice (www.thoughtrod.com) improves brainstorming.

Because the technology landscape is changing so rapidly, anything in a printed book would be outdated by the time it hit the bookstores. Therefore, I've created a page with the latest and greatest links to tools and other products that enable innovation. You can find it at www.stupidpractices.com/innovationtools.

APPENDIX B:

DISCOVER YOUR INNOVATION STYLE

In tip 26 ("Hire People You Don't Like"), the need for divergent points of view was discussed. And in particular I suggested that you should build teams with representation of every innovation style. If you are missing even one, your innovation efforts will suffer.

On the next page is a simple chart that can help you quickly assess the innovation style of each person on your team. You can download a copy of this from my Web site:

www.stupidpractices.com/innovationstyles

For each row, rank the words from most like you to least like you, where 1 represents most like you and 4 represents least like you.

For example, if you are very adventurous but not goal-oriented, you might rank the first row: intellectual 3, adventurous 1, goal-oriented 4, cheerleader 2.

A	B	C	D
Intellectual	Adventurous	Goal-Oriented	Cheerleader
Expert	Spontaneous	Driven	Diplomatic
Knowledgeable	Daring	Decisive	Sociable
Philosophical	Flexible	Direct	Gregarious
Discerning	Versatile	Competitive	Popular
Analytical	Creative	Disciplined	Nurturing
Logical	Visionary	Organized	Empathetic
Data Driven	Open Minded	Structured	Compassionate
Realistic	Insightful	Systematic	Loyal
Rational	Curious	Methodical	Considerate
Total	Total	Total	Total

SCORING YOUR INNOVATION STYLE QUIZ

To score, add the columns. The column with the *lowest* score is your style.

- If column A is the lowest, you are analytical and are driven by facts.
- If column B is the lowest, you like to generate creative ideas and engage in new experiences.
- If column C is the lowest, you prefer plans and actions.
- If column D is the lowest, your focus is on people.

Those from columns A and C are often called "left-brained" and are typically "dot" thinkers (see tip 32). They are great at challenging ideas and helping to drive toward solutions that are implementable and will add value. The risk is that these individuals can stifle innovation by overchallenging during the divergent stages of innovation.

Those from columns B and D are often referred to as "right-brained" and are typically "line" thinkers, as they are masterful at connecting dots. They are great at developing new concepts and engaging others in the process. The risk is that they may get lost in creativity for creativity's sake or worry too much about how others will feel, at the expense of powerful business solutions.

The innovation process goes from A to B to C to D. And although every style plays some role in each step, each style is best suited to one step in particular.

- *Define the Challenge*—This is best performed by the data-driven A's.
- *Generate Solutions*—the B's can help develop creative solutions.
- *Plan and Execute*—The methodical and goal-oriented C's will ensure progress.
- *Engage the Hearts and Minds*—The relationship-oriented D's can rally employees and customers so that everyone buys in and implements the solutions.

Each style is critical to the innovation process.

Go to www.PersonalityPokerBook.com to learn more about my Personality Poker card game. This will give you an even more accurate assessment of your team, in a highly interactive, collaborate, and fun way.

For those of you who have already played Personality Poker, the columns map to the suits as follows:

- Column A = spades
- Column B = diamonds
- Column C = clubs
- Column D = hearts

ACKNOWLEDGMENTS

For me, the acknowledgments are the most difficult part to write. Over the years, so many people have contributed concepts, comments, and content that ultimately made its way into this book. It would be impossible to thank everyone. But I do want to recognize a few people, realizing that so many others have made a contribution.

First and foremost, I want to thank my sister, Deborah Shapiro. She worked tirelessly (once again) around the clock to help make this book a reality. Without her, I am certain this would not have seen the light of day. I love her as a business colleague, book contributor, and an incredible friend.

I am honored to have Bonnie Solow as my literary agent. Her work goes well beyond the book. She serves as a sounding board, business adviser, and therapist.

A special thank you to Susanne Goldstein. When I needed someone to provide hypercritical feedback on an early version of the manuscript, she was happy to accommodate. She read the book cover to cover and provided incredible insights that immeasurably improved its readability. I can't thank you enough for your contribution to this book and to my life.

Although there are literally hundreds of people who have helped make this book possible, there are a few people in particular I would like to thank: Mick Simonelli and Janelle Dziuk from USAA; Dwayne Spradlin and Alph Bingham from Inno-Centive; Susan Baird and Larry Morse, both formerly with Quill Corporation; Katja Bressette; Scott Halford; Brad Kolar; Jason Bates; Adam Leffert; Mark Effinger; Michelle Joyce; Mark LeBlanc; and Dan Keldsen. Each knowingly—and in some cases unknowingly—contributed major pieces of content to this book.

I am thrilled to once again be published by Penguin's Portfolio imprint. Thank you Adrian Zackheim for deciding to publish this book. Emily Angell, I know you worked weekends and evenings to help birth this book. And thanks to Will Weisser, Jacquelynn Burke, Deb Lewis, and everyone else at Portfolio Penguin.

I would also like to thank my Accenture and InnoCentive colleagues, and my clients and friends who contributed over the years. It is through these experiences that I gather most of my stories.

Although he did not directly contribute to this book, a special shout-out is deserved by John Brunswick. He developed an amazing video game that brought my previous book, *Personality Poker*, to life on the Internet. You can check out his handiwork at game.personalitypokerbook.com.

And most important, on a personal note, I am eternally grateful to my parents for the love and support they have given me throughout my life. I have the perfect life because I have perfect parents. I am truly blessed.

NOTES

INTRODUCTION

- Julie Schmit, "After BP Oil Spill, Thousands of Ideas Poured in for Cleanup, *USA Today,* November 15, 2010; http://www.usatoday.com/money/industries/environment/2010-11-15-gulfcleanup15_CV_N.htm.

- E. B. Boyd, "Why Google's '20 Percent Time' Isn't Stemming Its Brain Drain, *Fast Company,* November 29, 2010; http://www.fastcompany.com/1706155/has-google-s-20-percent-time-met-its-limit.

- 3M Company, *A Century of 3M: The 3M Story* (3M Company, 2002). Available at http://multimedia.3m.com/mws/mediawebserver?mwsId=66666 UuZjcFSLXTtlxMt4xT6EVuQEcuZgVs6EVs6E666666—.

TIP 1

- Darwin is widely quoted as having said, "It is not the strongest of the species that survives, nor the most intelligent that survives. It is the one that is most adaptable to change." Interestingly, he never did. See http://www.darwinproject.ac.uk/six-things-darwin-never-said.

TIP 4

- A variation on the fifty-nine minutes quote is what Einstein said in 1938: "The mere formulation of a problem is far more often essential than its solution, which may be merely a matter of mathematical or experimental skill. To raise new questions, new possibilities, to regard old problems from a new angle requires creative imagination and marks real advances in science."

TIP 5

- Lee Fleming, "Breakthroughs and the 'Long Tail' of Innovation," *MIT Sloan Management Review,* fall 2007. Available at http://sloanreview.mit.edu/the-magazine/2007-fall/49114/breakthroughs-and-the-long-tail-of-innovation/.

- See http://www.netflixprize.com/.
- NASA challenges: National Innovation TRIZCON Conference, October 7–8, 2010, Dayton, Ohio.

TIP 9

- The actual quote from Edison was from an interview published in the January 1921 issue of *American Magazine:* "After we had conducted thousands of experiments on a certain project without solving the problem, one of my associates, after we had conducted the crowning experiment and it had proved a failure, expressed discouragement and disgust over our having failed to find out anything. I cheerily assured him that we had learned something. For we had learned for a certainty that the thing couldn't be done that way, and that we would have to try some other way."

TIP 10

- Christian Terwiesch and Karl Ulrich, *Innovation Tournaments* (Boston: Harvard Business School Press, 2009).
- For more on the Cisco I-Prize, see http://www.cisco.com/web/solutions/ iprize/index.html.
- For more on the LG Electronics competition, see http://www.crowd spring.com/project/2283311_lg-design-the-future-competition/access/.
- For more on GE ecomagination, see http://challenge.ecomagination.com/ home.
- For more on the X Prize, see http://space.xprize.org/ansari-x-prize.
- For more on the Pepsi Refresh Project, see http://www.refresheverything .com/.

TIP 11

- Kevin J. Boudreau and Karim R. Lakhani, "How to Manage Outside Innovation," *MIT Sloan Management Review,* July 1, 2009. Available at http:// sloanreview.mit.edu/the-magazine/articles/2009/summer/50413/how-to -manage-outside-innovation/.
- For more on the IBM Jam events, see https://www.collaborationjam .com/.
- Stephen Shapiro, *Personality Poker: The Playing Card Tool for Driving High-Performing Teamwork and Innovation* (New York: Portfolio Penguin, 2010).

TIP 12

• Saul Hansell, "Ideas Online, Yes, but Some Not So Presidential," *New York Times*, June 22, 2009. Available at http://www.nytimes.com/2009/06/23/technology/internet/23records.html?_r=2.

TIP 13

• Steven Spielberg, *Indiana Jones and the Last Crusade*, 1989.

TIP 14

• Anne Eisenberg, "The Hearing Aid as a Fashion Statement," *New York Times*, February 24, 2006.

• Kendall Haven, *Story Proof: The Science Behind the Startling Power of Story* (Westport, CT: Libraries Unlimited, 2007).

• For more on the Zaltman Metaphor Elicitation Technique (ZMET), see http://www.olsonzaltman.com/.

• For more on the Accenture study, see http://www.slideshare.net/AccentureNL/accenture-innovation-awards-2010-communications-high-tech (slide 3).

TIP 15

• Barry Schwartz, "When Words Decide," *Scientific American Mind*, August/September 2007. Available at http://www.sciamdigital.com/index.cfm?fa=Products.ViewIssuePreview&ARTICLEID_CHAR=094D406E-3048-8A5E-10A109B5CE9BC955.

• Ellen Florian, "The Money Machines: The Humble ATM Revolutionized the Way We Deal with Money and Turned Global Commerce into a 24/7 Affair. You Can Thank a Texan Named Don Wetzel—and the Blizzard of 1978," *Fortune*, July 26, 2004. Available at http://money.cnn.com/magazines/fortune/fortune_archive/2004/07/26/377172/index.htm.

• The dust mite fact has been debunked. See http://www.straightdope.com/columns/read/2545/does-a-mattress-double-its-weight-due-to-dust-mites-and-their-debris.

TIP 19

• The video game facts come from http://www.xbitlabs.com/news/multimedia/display/20090211133015_Nintendo_Wii_Continues_to_Dominate_Console_Market_Xbox_360_Stagnates_PlayStation_3_Becomes_Victim_of_Economic_Recession.html.

TIP 20

- Chip Conley, *Peak: How Great Companies Get Their Mojo from Maslow* (San Francisco: Jossey-Bass, 2007).

TIP 22

- Dan Pink, *Drive: The Surprising Truth About What Motivates Us* (New York: Riverhead Hardcover, 2009).
- Yerkes Dodson: http://en.wikipedia.org/wiki/Yerkes–Dodson_law.
- Beth A. Hennessey and Teresa M. Amabile, "Creativity," first published online as a Review in Advance on October 19, 2009. The *Annual Review of Psychology* is online at psych.annualreviews.org. This article's doi: 10 .1146/annurev.psych.093008.100416.

TIP 24

- "How Failure Breeds Success," *BusinessWeek*, July 10, 2006. Available at http://www.businessweek.com/magazine/content/06_28/b3992001 .htm.
- Charles Koch, *The Science of Success: How Market-Based Management Built the World's Largest Private Company* (Hoboken, NJ: Wiley, 2007).

TIP 25

- Playbook: Best Practices, BusinessWeek Online, http://www.business week.com/magazine/content/06_28/b3992001.htm.
- Martin A. Tolcott and F. Freeman Marvin, "Reducing the Confirmation Bias in an Evolving Situation," United States Army Research Institute for the Behavioral and Social Sciences, February 1995. http://www.dtic.mil/ cgi-bin/GetTRDoc?Location=U2&doc=GetTRDoc.pdf&AD=ADA293570.

TIP 26

- Clint A. Bowers, James A. Pharmer, and Eduardo Salas, "When Member Homogeneity Is Needed in Work Teams: A Meta- Analysis," *Small Group Research* 31 (2000): 305–27.
- S. Barsade, A. Ward, J. Turner, and J. Sonnenfeld, "To Your Heart's Content: A Model of Affective Diversity in Top Management Teams," *Administrative Science Quarterly* 45 (2000): 802–36.

TIP 28

- Traci Fenton, "Democracy in the Workplace," *Christian Science Monitor*, August 23, 2006. Available at http://www.csmonitor.com/2006/0823/p09s01-coop.html.
- Traci Fenton, "Change Your Operating System," *Conference Board Review*, September 2010. Available at http://www.tcbreview.com/if-you-love-your-people-set-them-free.php.

TIP 38

- George Land and Beth Jarman, *Breaking Point and Beyond* (New York: HarperBusiness, 1993).

INDEX